AMERICA

An Illustrated Diary of Its
of Its
Most Exciting Years

PRESS

A division of American Family Enterprises, Inc.

Robert Schramke—Publisher
Alan C. Hahn—Marketing Director
Robert Whiteman—Editorial Consultant
Marilyn Appleberg—Managing Editor
Louis Fulgoni—Book Design
Susan McQuibben—Picture Research

The Stonehouse Press—Production Supervision

PHOTO CREDITS

Page 10, 11, Robert Weaver; 12, Underwood & Underwood; 15, 17, Brown Bros.; 18, Bettman Archive; 19, (top) Brown Bros.; (btm.)
UPI; 20, Culver Pictures; 21, Brown Bros.; 22, Robert Weaver; 24, Frederick Lewis; 25, Bettman Archive; 26, courtesy of NBC; 27,
Bettman Archive; 28, (top) Granger Collection; (btm.) Brown Bros.; 29, Granger Collection; 30, 31, courtesy of NBC; 32, Frederick
Lewis; 33, Bettman Archive; 34, Granger Collection; 35, (top) Frederick Lewis; 35, (btm.) 36, 37, courtesy of NBC; 38, courtesy of
CBS; 39, (top) Frederick Lewis; (btm.) courtesy of CBS; 40, 41, 43, 45, Brown Bros.; 46, UPI; 48, Brown Bros.; 49, 52, Wide World; 53,
Brown Bros.; 54, 55, Mel Greifinger; 57, Brown Bros.; 60, Robert Weaver; 62, 63, Brown Bros.; 65, Wide World; 66, Underwood &
Underwood; 67, Brown Bros.; 69, UPI; 70, Robert Weaver; 71, Brown Bros.; 72, Wide World; 73, UPI; 75, Robert Weaver; 76,
Wide World; 78, 80, 81, 82, Brown Bros.; 84, Wide World; 87, UPI; 89, Brown Bros.; 91, Bettman Archive; 93, 94, Brown Bros.; 97,
Wide World; 98, Granger Collection; 100, Wide World; 102, courtesy of NBC; 104, 105, Brown Bros.; 106, Robert Weaver; 108,
Underwood & Underwood; 109, (top) Bettman Archive; (btm) UPI; 110, 111, 112, Brown Bros.; 114, Bettman Archive; 116, 118, 120,
122, Judy Mitchell; 124, Wide World; 127, Brown Bros.; 128, Granger Collection; 130, Brown Bros.; 133, 135, Underwood &
Underwood; 134, Robert Weaver; 136, 140, 141, UPI. Endleaves: Bettman Archive; Brown Bros.; Cinemabilia; Culver Pictures;
Frederick Lewis; Granger Collection; Movie Star News; Library of Congress; UPI.

Printed in the United States of America

Table of Contents

FOREWORD

For thousands of years mankind has relegated the task of recording the most important events to historians. In most instances, these men have been "third parties" who would set down the facts as they viewed them, or even as they thought they occurred. It is interesting, therefore, when one finds a page of history or even a period documented by the people that actually made it happen. The world comes to life when Roosevelt and Churchill discuss political decisions, Babe Ruth and Lou Gehrig talk about hitting, Ethel Barrymore and Helen Hayes tell of their stage experiences.

This is AMERICA, A DIARY OF ITS MOST EXCITING YEARS. The sights, sounds and even the mood of the United States, and the world, is conveyed to us in this new and exciting series of books.

The period from 1914 through 1960 is perhaps the most significant in all of our history and it is these years that have been chosen by the Editorial Staff to be the framework for this set. On almost any day of the week one could find people and events taking place that have changed our world as in no other period in history. Two major world wars were fought, a depression came and went, the airplane and television were invented. Even the very lifestyle of America changed. We stopped working 15 hours a day and had time to relax and think. The movies, radio and television brought entertainment into our lives, sports became a necessary part of our daily discussions and we changed. From an insecure, developing young country into the major world power, America has transformed itself in just 50 years.

It is this transformation that you will see, and be a part of again. In this first volume of AMERICA, you will find exciting examples of what future volumes in this series will offer. We hope you will enjoy this introductory volume and all those to follow.

The Editors

GANGSTERS AND GANGBUSTERS

Crime was the nation's front-page sensation back in the Nineteen Twenties. Not the sort of street crime we know today, but a lawlessness organized by clever criminal elements who banded together in the country's cities to take advantage of the Prohibition Law which went into effect in January 1920. After a brief moment of surprise that this law had actually gone on the books, the people decided they still wanted to drink—but how to get what was then called booze or hooch? The answer was to buy it illicitly and so emerged rum runners, bootleggers, speakeasies and gang wars. Ghetto-bred gangsters spawned by Prohibition took over city streets, gunning down rival hoods, sometimes killing innocent bystanders. Police and public rose in protest, but rum-running was so lucrative that the crime wave of the Twenties could not be stopped. Names like Scarface Al Capone and Legs Diamond became as well known as that of the President of the United States. Throughout the Roaring Twenties, crime roared louder than anything else.

Earl "Hymie" Weiss is carried to his Maker.

The Twilight of the Gangster

by Edward Doherty

Edward Doherty, who wrote this article in 1929, was a star reporter on the Chicago Tribune's crime-hunting team. He also wrote for national magazines like the Saturday Evening Post, Collier's, and Liberty.

We, the people of the United States, are a queer lot—perhaps the queerest in the world. We're as paradoxical as an Irish bull. But we have our moments! We call America the Cradle of Liberty, and vote it dry. We boast of our courage, and let criminals run us and rob us and kill us.

We've created a host of robber barons in the last ten years. We've let them amass enormous riches. We've let them pillage and slay. We've pampered and petted them. We've made them idols. We've cheered Alphonse "Scar-face" Capone every time he was acquitted. We've cried "Persecution!" every time he went on trial. We've cheered Jack "Legs" Diamond when he was acquitted of burning the feet of a man he was charged with kidnaping.

We let them go their ways. We let them establish themselves. We let them become powerful. We let them use our streets for slaughterhouses, let them turn machine guns loose on our busiest thoroughfares.

Innocent people have been killed, wounded, maimed for life—men and women and little children at play. Our rivers and our highways have been used for the dumping of grotesque bullet-riddled bodies.

We jailed women who sold a few bottles of whisky or home brew. Officers have shot down men who were carrying pint bottles of illicit liquor. We have hanged or electrocuted kids who made our feudal heroes their heroes, and who went out with guns to rob or to kill.

But have we hanged or electrocuted any of our feudal bootleg dukes?

Scalice and Anselmi, killers imported from Sicily to help Capone and the Genna brothers in Chicago, were convicted of killing two policemen and wounding a third. But what happened? They were acquitted.

Strange they should come from Sicily? Not at all. Sicily, the home of the Mafia, harbored the deadliest assassins in the world until the "despotic" Mussolini cleared Italy of its criminals. He jailed a lot. He killed a lot. But many of them are over here now—serving feudal liquor lords and getting rich.

Never in the history of the United States has there been such public flouting of law and order as we have permitted in the last ten years.

Hymie Weiss once took a cavalcade of motor cars past a hotel in Cicero, Illinois, a suburb of Chicago, and turned its walls into a huge Swiss cheese. The rest of the world was appalled. But America was phlegmatic. It was just a gangster gesture.

Weiss, affectionately known as "Little Hymie," lived to boast about that exploit. He lived three weeks.

Capone's machine gunners massacred seven men in a Chicago garage. Two of the murderers were dressed in the uniforms of policemen. America began to be shocked. A joke was a joke, but this was carrying a joke too far.

But what could be done about it? Everybody knew Capone had planned that massacre. But he was immune.

"Well," we said, "somebody will get Capone." And we let it go at that. A well-fed, busy, moneymaking America could forget a massacre and continue to wink at gangsters.

Gangsters Deglamorized

But now the glamour has been stripped from the gangsters. Even the most stupid of us see them now as they are, yellow louts, red-handed plunderers. We have begun to realize they have waged actual war upon us in this last red decade.

And young America, growing to manhood, is following their example.

13

Last August two nineteen-year-old boys, carrying a small arsenal with them, held up a payroll messenger, stole over $4,000 from him, shot the police guard dead, and fled in a taxicab. A motorcycle policeman tried to stop them. They killed him too!

And then the new feeling in America showed itself.

Vincent Hyde, a fireman, picked up the motorcycle policeman's pistol and cartridge belt, jumped on the running board of another cab, and gave chase. He fired at the fugitives until he dropped, wounded. Rubin Katz, that taxi's driver, though he had a wound in the throat, never faltered until the fleeing car crashed against a truck. The police showed their heroism too, as they always do in emergencies. There were cops on the running boards of every car in the pursuit, targets for the bullets of the two kids in the taxicab ahead. Six were killed in that chase, including the bandits, their driver, and a little girl who was sitting with her father and mother in an automobile.

She was the second child killed within a month in the city of New York.

The man who drove the kids who tried to ape the gangster kings was Herbert Hasse. He seems to have been a hard-working, decent chap, a typical American citizen. He had a wife, a family. Gunmen probably didn't mean anything to him. Let them alone and they'll let you alone, he might have told you. Or he might have said, "Well, we got to get our booze somewhere, and those guys only kill each other."

The bandits jumped into his car. It might have been yours. Any car will do for a bandit making an escape. They put a gun to Hasse's head and made him speed. He didn't want to, no doubt. But he didn't want to die. His family needed him. Somebody shot Hasse dead.

If those two boys had been real gangsters, out for some quick money—and gangsters do not hesitate to rob—they would not have killed the policemen intentionally. Gangsters are careful about killing cops—they want cops to protect them. They need police friendship.

But even if they were gangsters they wouldn't have hesitated a moment to kill every *civilian* man, woman, and child who got in their way.

It isn't so long since Vincent Coll's men,

hunting an enemy in Manhattan, turned a machine gun loose in a street crowded with children. They riddled a baby buggy, and the slugs tore through the body of a sleeping child and killed him. Four other children were left lying on the sidewalk, unconscious or screaming with pain, before the gun was silenced and the car drove off.

Declaration of War

Commissioner Mulrooney in New York City and Commissioner Alcock in Chicago have declared war on gangsters, real war. Mulrooney has told his men to shoot first, and shoot above the waistline. And he means it.

Governor Franklin D. Roosevelt of New York did his best to send Jack Diamond to jail. He failed. A crowd cheered when Diamond was acquitted. Jack Diamond, "the clay pigeon of gangdom," "the big shot," "the much shot at," thief and murderer that he is, was cheered as though he were a national hero.

But the federal government doesn't think him a hero. It tried him in New York, and convicted him of conspiring to violate the prohibition law and of owning a still. Judge Richard J. Hopkins of Kansas gave him the limit—four years and a fine of $11,000—and directed that he be prosecuted under the Jones law.

"Under that law," the judge said, "he might be sentenced to thirty or forty years."

Paul Quattrocchi, one of Diamonds's lieutenants, was sentenced with him. Diamond has appealed, and is at liberty pending a hearing on the appeal. But jail seems certain for him—unless sombody saves him with a machine gun.

Capone is going to jail too. He has been indicted by a federal grand jury. He is accused of income-tax frauds and of 5,000 specific violations of the prohibition law. Sixty-eight of his vassals are named with him. It is charged that his syndicate's income from beer alone totaled $75,000 a day.

Capone had it all fixed, he thought, to make a bargain with the prosecution. He'd plead guilty and spend a few years in a nice jail where he could have every luxury. But Federal Judge James Wilkerson wouldn't bargain with him. Capone withdrew his plea of guilty, and he and his lawyer are talking things over. But, rest assured, Capone is going to jail. Judge Wilkerson sentenced him to thirty days for contempt of court last winter. He hasn't served that term yet. But he will. Unless—as in Diamond's case—some machine gunner catches him first.

The twilight of the gangs! Capone and Diamond will go to jail. Coll will go to the chair if he's found. "Dutch" Schultz is done as a big shot since his arrest. This despite his acquittal. "Waxy" Gordon, Vannie Higgins, "Bugs" Moran—all the feudal princelings you can mention are wondering what will happen to them.

Gangland Justice

Look at Capone, who is reputed to have had $60,000,000. He's in fear of his life every moment. He's guarded by a hundred men constantly. He rides in an armored car. His guards surround him when he's at a theater, or a prize fight, or in any crowd. He wakes up every little while and goes to another bed —he has many beds—so an assassin will have a hard time finding him. He doesn't trust any of his guards. He dares not. He once trusted Anselmi and Scalice.

He was told that Anselmi and Scalice had ambitions. They wanted to be rid of him and join forces with Joe Giunta, whom Capone had made head of the Unione Siciliano.

Capone sent two men to test Anselmi. They found Anselmi ready to betray his king. They agreed to help him.

"Don't use your gun," one of them said. "That can be identified. I'll get you one. Wait here." He went into another room, shook the cartridges out of his revolver, removed the bullets, and put the empty shells back into the chambers.

Anselmi went upstairs, the gun in his hand. He went into Capone's office. Capone stood with his back to Anselmi. Anselmi fired twice. The pin clicked on two empty shells. Anselmi turned pale and put the gun away.

Capone turned. He appeared to have noticed nothing. He greeted Anselmi with a beaming smile. He shook hands with Anselmi. He embraced him.

"I am giving a big dinner tonight for you and Scalice and Giunta," he said. "I'll have all the rest of the boys there, but you three will be guests of honor."

The banquet was held in a roadhouse south of Chicago. All the guests were searched and frisked as they came in.

Scalice, Anselmi, and Giunta ate heartily and drank well. Perhaps they knew what was to happen. If they didn't they were fools.

Capone got up at last and drank a toast to them, and made them stand in the middle of the floor. Then two men who had proved their loyalty to the king drew guns and told the guests of honor to line up against the wall.

"Here are three fine traitors," Capone said. He revealed their treachery. He reviled them in bitter words. Then he advanced slowly toward them, holding a baseball bat in his hands. He clubbed each one to death, and his men filled their bodies full of bullet holes.

"That's how we punish traitors," said Capone. "Throw them in some ditch in Indiana."

Capone may still have $60,000,000, but his life is one great nightmare of fear—the fear of being killed.

Capone fled from Brooklyn to Chicago years ago, to escape arrest. He lay low for a long

A mug-shot of "Scarface" Al Capone.

time in the Chicago underworld. He was known as Al Brown. Johnny Torrio, who had known him in NEW York, taught him the art of murder. "Big Jim" Colosimo, the boss of the underworld, used him as a messenger boy, cursed and kicked him.

Big Jim was told that a load of booze would be delivered to him one afternoon, and he was to pay for it with cash. He had the money on him when he was killed. The killer got it. Johnny Torrio took over Colosimo's kingdom, and added to it joints all around Chicago.

Johnny Torrio and Al Capone had Dion O'Banion killed. Two men shook hands with him in his flower shop across from the Holy Name Cathedral; and while they held his hands, a third man pumped him full of lead.

George "Bugs" Moran, one of O'Banion's most fanatic friends, shot Torrio in the neck, and sent him screaming to a hospital. He was never any good to the racket after that. And Capone was king in his place.

Guarded but Fearful

One of the first things Capone did was to guard his person well. He brought in bandits who had fled the wrath of Mussolini. Mafiosi from Sicily, Camorristas from Neapolitan streets and alleys.

But, though they guarded him well, he was still afraid. He was afraid of Bugs Moran. He was afraid of the crazy Earl Hymie Weiss, of "Polack" Joe Saltis, of the red-faced McErlane. He was afraid of the O'Donnells.

He had good reason to fear Hymie Weiss, for that desperado had declared war on Capone "and all them greaseballs," and also he had bought a lot of machine guns. Weiss was the first of the bootleggers to use that weapon.

Every so often he went looking for Capone —but Capone had made himself hard to find. Hymie had neither guile nor imagination. He took a long time to make up his mind. But once he had made his plan—and it was usually the craziest he could think of—he executed it at once.

Capone had grown up to learn about forks and caviar and opera. Society women raved about the wistfulness of his voice. Weiss had remained a roughneck.

Capone kept himself in Cicero or in Florida. Weiss ruled the Chicago Loop, and made his headquarters over Dion O'Banion's flower shop across from the cathedral.

Capone tendered the olive branch to his enemies. They talked peace terms in a downtown restaurant. Weiss got very drunk—but when he sobered he doubted that Capone wanted peace, and determined to give him hell.

He learned that the Genna brothers, allies of Capone, were having him followed—him and all the other enemies of Capone. Chicago was full of Gennas, it seemed to Weiss. They were alky cookers. They employed hundreds of their countrymen to cook alky and sold it to Capone. They were rich—and getting powerful. Several high public officials attended one of their banquets.

Weiss put a police gong on one of his autos and went out hunting Gennas. He got Angelo first. And later he bagged Anthony. A cop got Mike—wounded him fatally after he and Anselmi and Scalice had killed two detectives. Jim Genna wasn't tricked by the sound of the gong into thinking Weiss was only a cop. He beat it back to Sicily. The other Gennas stayed in their homes until they could safely sneak to some spot far from Chicago.

There were more than 15,000 alky-cooking places in Chicago at the time. The Gennas owned all those on the North Side. They made millions of dollars selling this stuff—the basis of gin and whiskies. They used to "kick in" about $6,000 or $7,000 a month to be "let alone."

Angelo, who was the head of the Unione Siciliano—ostensibly a patriotic American-Italian society, but actually a union of alky cookers, bootleggers, and killers—had slain many men before he came to power. Weiss got him shortly after he married, killed him when he was rich and happy and respected and feared.

Motorized Murder

Weiss was one of the first to organize murder on wheels—steal a car, fill it full of trigger men, and go cruising around until an enemy was sighted, then "give him the bang" and tear through the streets to safety.

He got Angelo that way. Angelo was in his own powerful new car. Weiss' machine came up from behind. The guns roared. Angelo stepped on the gas and the car tore through

Chicago's streets like a scared rabbit. Weiss' car followed like a greyhound. Angelo tried to turn a corner quickly. His car skidded into a lamp-post—and the machine guns laughed as he screamed for mercy.

Weiss had to use treachery on Anthony. Anthony wouldn't go out of his house for anyone save his very good friend Antonio Spano—whom the Gennas had imported from their native town, Marsala, Sicily. Spano was known as "the Cavalier."

Weiss found the Cavalier and held a gun to his head, and bade him telephone Anthony and put him on the spot.

"Talk all the spiggoty you want," he advised the Cavalier. "The guy with me is a wop. Talk wop to him, Luigi. Luigi will understand everything you say."

Anthony Genna met Antonio Spano on the corner Weiss had designated. He greeted him effusively. Spano held his hands tightly, as a friend should. And Weiss fired.

A Genna died as O'Banion had died.

Anthony was shot in the back. He lived just long enough to breathe the name of his betrayer, the Cavalier.

Hymie Blasted

Hymie was satisfied for a time. He would get Capone, but he'd have to wait. Meantime he had to help his fellow Pole, Joe Saltis. Saltis and Lefty Koncil were on trial for the murder of "Mitters" Foley.

Hymie attended every session of the trial. He put everything he had into the task of saving Joe—and so forgot to be careful.

He had no idea that six Sicilian machine gunners were waiting patiently for him to walk before their guns. They had spent days waiting. There was a machine-gun nest across from the cathedral—with three men working in eight-hour shifts. There was another nest on the corner.

Those six gunners must have heard the ringing of vesper bells, the resonant sound of the organ, the voices of the choir, the chorus of the pious repeating the words of litanies. Perhaps they even joined in the chant at times, since there was nothing better to do.

Weiss left court with his bodyguard, Pat Murray, and picked up Attorney W. W. O'Brien and his investigator, Ben Jacobs. Sam Peller drove the car. They parked the machine at the corner of the cathedral shortly after three P.M.; and the gun in the nest across the street immediately came to life. Weiss and Murray dropped dead. The other three were wounded. More than fifty slugs are still in the cornerstone of the church.

What did it profit Earl Hymie Weiss to be a bootleg king with power of life and death? There was a certain glamour about him because of his loyalty to the memory of his friend O'Banion. But was it brave to kill Angelo Genna when he was helpless? Was it brave to shoot Anthony Genna in the back while a traitor held his hands? Was it brave to take a small army of armored cars into Cicero and shoot up Capone's hotel? He had glamour, but he was a coward and a fool.

Incidentally, he wounded a woman during that silly one-sided battle in Cicero. He wouldn't have cared if he had killed her and a dozen others. She was in the path of his machine-gun bullets. It was just too bad. That was all. She had no business walking the street when a gangster king was out for a bit of murder.

They only kill each other—and any innocent man or woman or child who gets in their way.

Dillinger Dies!
by Will Irwin

Will Irwin bears one of the most illustrious names in American journalism. As a young reporter, he covered the San Francisco earthquake and wrote of it so memorably that his dispatches appear in journalism anthologies and text books. Still a crack working reporter in 1933, Mr. Irwin wrote this dramatic account of John Dillinger.

This is how Uncle Sam's police—whom the underworld calls the "G-men"—cornered and killed that poisonous little rat John Dillinger, to the satisfaction of all.

On the afternoon of Sunday, July 22, J. Edgar Hoover, who directs the Division of Criminal Investigation, Department of Justice, sat in his Washington home, reading a frivolous novel and taking his rest after a hard week. The telephone rang. He had given instructions that he was to be disturbed only in case of really important business; and even before he lifted the receiver his mind said, "Dillinger." For three months the little force of federal agents had been pursuing that elusive killer through a maze of hard luck. Four times they had almost cornered him; and each time fate had played on his side. His hairbreadth escapes, his weird luck, had made him a symbol of defiance for law.

And Dillinger's name, disguised in a rough-and-ready code, was the first word to come over the wire. Agent M. H. Purvis was speaking from Chicago. "He is going to the movies tonight," said Purvis in code. "Either the Marboro Theater or the Biograph. He'll have two women with him. The boys are looking over the land right now. We'll get him when he goes in or when he comes out. Wish us luck, and good-bye!" And Hoover settled down to the most anxious six hours of his life.

Purvis had to cover both theaters, but the Biograph more closely than the Marboro. For it was showing a gangster film, and they knew Dillinger's tastes. The human instinct was to fill

A snapshot of Dillinger posing with the "tools" of his trade.

the environs with plain-clothes men. But Dillinger, that creature of instincts, would take alarm if he saw an unusual number of men loafing about the theater. Moreover, shooting by a large posse might turn into a fusillade; and Purvis found himself more concerned with the lives of women and children crowding in and out of the theater than with his own life and that of his agents. Three or four men at each theater, dead shots all, would be enough. The police of East Chicago, Indiana, bent on avenging a comrade whom Dillinger had murdered in cold blood, were following his trail amost as closely as the federal men and had given invaluable help. They deserved a place in this operation. If Dillinger showed signs of resisting arrest, each man was to shoot only once—and to the spot.

So, when the crowds began entering the Biograph and the Marboro, four men loafed inconspicuously about each entrance. Purvis himself was at the Biograph. Neither he nor his associates had ever seen the enemy in the flesh. But Purvis had studied Dillinger's face in photographs and newsreels until he felt that he knew him like a brother.

A little man escorting two women stepped to the box office. He was in his shirt sleeves, for it was a hot night; but he wore a straw hat. Dillinger! Or was it? He was wearing spectacles, and the face seemed oddly changed. Then he spoke, and Purvis caught a characteristic expression which he had noted in the newsreels—caught it a tenth of a second too late. The Sunday night crowd pushed in close. Shooting would mean a massacre. Before an opening appeared, Dillinger and his two girls had entered the theater. A delay. (In Washington, Mr. Hoover was walking the floor, consulting his watch every five minutes.) They would get him when he came out.

A messenger brought over the force from the Marboro. Quietly Purvis deployed his troops; at the entrance, he and two other federal agents; at the curb, one federal agent and the East Chicago policemen. After an interminable wait the audience began to emerge. Purvis lighted a cigar. Here he was—Dillinger! Purvis dropped his cigar. That was the signal. Dillinger's animal intuition stayed with him to the end. The motion had occurred behind him—but he glanced nervously over his shoulder and his right hand shot to the automatic pistol in the pocket of his trousers. It caught in the vent of the pocket. He jammed it down to get it free— and three shots exploded almost as one. Staggering, glassy-eyed, bleeding, he ran down the street toward an alley. The squad at the curb closed in. But it would not be necessary to fire again. At the entrance of the alley he pitched forward on his face. In twenty minutes he was dead.

He had been hit three times in different spots. The federal men had thought out even that detail before hand. Traditionally, the safest plan for a man in a life-and-death gun fight is to aim at the heart. Even if you miss a trifle, you've probably inflicted a fatal or disabling wound. The bulletproof vest has somewhat altered that rule. Dillinger might be wearing armor under his shirt. So one marksman had fired at his torso, one at his head, and one at his leg, so that he could not run away. All hit the mark. The woman bystander wounded in the fracas took a bullet which went clean through Dillinger. As for the men behind the guns— "Never mind," said Director Hoover at the time. "They have families." However, we know now that agents Hollis and Cowley, who four months later died heroically while ridding us of "Baby Face" Nelson, were in the federal squad.

At half past ten Hoover's telephone rang again. Chicago was speaking: "We've got him— he's dead!"

"Any of our boys killed?"

"Not one! A woman in the crowd wounded, but not badly, we think."

"Thank God!"

Dillinger, in one of his rare court appearances, is handcuffed to a court officer.

Bonnie and Clyde by Will Irwin

In addition to the Dillinger account, Irwin also wrote this short commentary on the death of Bonnie Parker and Clyde Barrow.

When they weren't on the run, Bonnie and Clyde would practice their marksmanship.

Clyde and Buck Barrow, together with Bonnie Parker, Clyde's lurid light-o'-love, were the first to shoot their way into national notoriety. Let us look at them as they were—we have of late hung too many romantic trimmings upon thugs and morons of this sort. The Barrows were mental, moral, and physical scrubs. Buck measured five feet five inches in height; Clyde, the worse of the pair, five feet three. Neither weighed much more than 100 pounds.

Parenthetically, most of the really dangerous characters whose Bertillon measurements decorate the criminal archives at Washington rate in the flyweight class. Any modern psychologist will tell you that this is no accident. The scrubby little boy with criminal tendencies has in his childhood stood for bullying and persecution by other little boys. When he grows up and goes on the loose, he has a complex of physical inferiority; and he compensates for it by brutality with those instruments which made dwarfs stand equal to giants—guns.

The bodies of the Barrows were colossal compared to their souls. I need cite only one instance. Getting away from a robbery, they needed a car. They found one in possession of a farmer's wife. Even when she faced a gun, she objected to handing over the keys. Whereupon they knocked her out with a chain and assaulted her criminally before they went their way.

From small holdups at filling stations they passed on to bank robberies. Rather early in the game, a posse shot at Buck. He died miserably a few weeks later from infection in his wounds. Clyde and Bonnie Parker carried on. She was a blonde with a hard mouth who smoked black cigars, had herself photographed guns in hand, and shot as well as her man. When hiding out in the wilds they practiced their shooting constantly—and photographed each other standing beside their targets. Except for a sentimental streak in Bonnie which moved her to write atrocious poetry, vanity was the only human trait they possessed.

Gradually the posses hunting them grew larger and larger. Once Governor Murray of Oklahoma called out four companies of militia and all the deputies in four or five counties. Sometime they sneaked through the cordons; just as often, they got away by accurate fast shooting with machine guns or automatics. Before they died they had at least a dozen murders on their souls. Most of the victims were police officers doing their duty. One murder reveals again what kind of people these Barrows were. They had held up a grocer in the presence of his wife. He hoisted his hands and made no resistance while they stripped his till. Then, as they turned away, one of them shot him dead—" just for luck."

Both Clyde Barrow and Bonnie Parker took several wounds in their brushes with the law. They sneaked at last into the remote bayou country of Louisiana. Sheriff Henderson Jordon of Bienville Parish, learning of their presence from federal agents, formed a posse, laid a clever trap, annihilated them with automatic rifles and machine guns. He said afterward that he loathed the thought of killing a woman; but what else could a responsible officer of the law do with a Bonnie Parker?

A gun made up for Clyde Barrow's lack of physical stature.

FROM VAUDEVILLE TO TELEVISION

Gods and Goddesses, that's what we made of them . . .

Yes, motion pictures, then radio, brought something new to the country—a chance for every American to worship handsome men and beautiful women, and laugh along with the funny ones. We could also spend a lot of time wondering how these glamorous folk lived and loved.

Then came television, and we could all but invite the glamorous people into our living rooms.

Yes, we made Gods and Goddesses of our movie stars, our airwaves talents, our picture-screen lovers.

But what were they like, really? In this montage of words and pictures we try to show that it's impossible to generalize about the lives of entertainment luminaries. Some were (or are) happy; others tragic, for reasons hard to figure out. Why, for instance, did Jean Harlow die in her twenties, and Marilyn Monroe kill herself. Didn't there two lovely girls have it made? We thought so.

Why is Garbo a loner, who flees when admirers approach? Why was W. C. Fields, with so much money in the bank, a man in constant fear? Or Charlie Chaplin so pleased with himself . . . And so on.

We'll never know the true answers, but we can always guess. Perhaps this potpourri of pieces will help in the guessing games.

Florenz Ziegfeld (1927)

Florenz Ziegfeld rose from an apprenticeship with Buffalo Bill's Wild West Show to become one of the greatest names in modern entertainment. He knew the value of showmanship and to that end he reproduced the dreams of the average American on the Broadway stage.

The Ziegfeld Follies were the greatest stage spectaculars of the time. Gorgeous girls were dressed in lavish costumes and sets were created costing hundreds of thousands of dollars. The musical scores were written by only the best composers, Irving Berlin, Jerome Kern and Victor Herbert to name a few.

Even comedy had a place in his shows as evidenced by the fact that W.C. Fields, Ed Wynn, Eddie Cantor and Will Rogers all worked in some editions of the Follies.

Future movie starlets also got a helping hand in his review. Paulette Goddard, Irene Dunne, Barbara Stanwyck are just a few of the gals that eventually made their mark in show business.

Florenz Ziegfeld had style and it was apparent in everything he did, on stage and off. He would telegram rather than call people, travel in his own private railroad car, and spend any amount of money to make an impression.

A showman in the greatest sense, he created a concept in stage entertainment that was often imitated but never equaled.

The Ziegfeld girls as they appeared on stage at the Follies.

Rudolph Valentino (1929)

Rudolph Valentino is dead.

Death found the lonely sheik of the screen fighting to keep his place on the front pages. Even while he was struggling for life, his critics whispered cynically: "Publicity!"

I am not sure but that death saved Valentino from a greater tragedy—the forgetfulness of the public. The Valentino vogue had waned. The Son of the Sheik was an effort to revive a past popularity. Oblivion might have been just around the corner.

Frustration stalked Valentino at every turn. At the zenith of his film career, he became involved in legal difficulties with his producers, Famous Players. This forced him to remain off the screen for a long period. Then, at the height of his attempt to win back his old position, came death.

Valentino migrated to Hollywood from the tango *dansantes*. He hit sudden success with his *Julio* in The Four Horsemen. The puzzled, naive Italian boy was lifted to the heights. He became an international vogue—and lost his head. Valentino's marriages, his affairs of the heart, his embroidered silk bath robes, his slave bracelet became front page gossip.

The Sheik spent his money extravagantly. He purchased an elaborate Beverly Hills home. He bought prize riding horses and imported cars with silver snakes crawling around the hoods. The boy who had polished brass in New York car barns a few years before was tasting life with a lavish gesture.

Perhaps there was a prophetic note in the way the walls of Valentino's Beverly Hills house began to crack and collapse last spring. Valentino called in Hollywood's best builders to save his home, just as he called in the best publicity men to save his career.

Before his death, Rudy's screen career scared Hollywood and made popularity a bug-bear. "Heaven help me from becoming as popular as Valentino," Jack Gilbert told friends.

Filmdom had drawn the inference that the public is a sort of Catherine the Great, quick to love, eager to reward, and happy to forget.

Rudolph Valentino in "Son of the Sheik"

Valentino, however, sacrificed his popularity because he never quite understood.

Rudolph Valentino violated all the rules of the film game. He married not once but twice. Film fans like their idols unmarried. When Richard Barthelmess recently separated from his wife, his "fan mail" doubled instantly.

Valentino quarreled with his bosses and was banned legally from the screen because of contract difficulties. Then he started his tour on behalf of a beauty mud.

The Sheik had stepped from his pedestal and the public never quite forgave him.

The star of the Four Horsemen made fortunes for his various employers, but had little when death came, despite the various newspaper reports of the $1,000,000 estate he left. He received $1,000,000 for making The Son of the Sheik. But what was that sum, checked against litigations and all the expenses of a cinema favorite?

What shall I say of The Son of the Sheik? It would have been his biggest money maker since The Sheik. Now, it's just the epilogue of a frustrated career.

25

Gloria Swanson (1929)

The great Gloria Swanson comments on one aspect of silent film acting.

"I wish there were some way of *seeing* instead of reading it or hearing it. Language causes more trouble in choosing a story than anything else. An author may describe a character beautifully, so that she becomes alive on the page. But, for the character to be alive on the screen, she must act. And very often an action that seems perfectly logical on the printed page, camouflaged by an exquisite choice of words, or even sufficiently obscured by commonplace words in an ordinary script, becomes impractical, or out of keeping, or awkward, or ridiculous, before the camera.

"She crossed the wide room slowly, trailing her draperies. At the door she paused and bent over a fragrant bowl of roses on a side table. The clear summer sky through the French windows caught her eye and she stood lost in contemplation of one white, fleecy cloud wafted across it. After a moment she sighed and went wearily from the room.

"So says the writer. In a few sentences he sets his scene. Think what it would mean on the screen—the elegance of the wide room costing several thousand dollars, the furnishings and the draperies, not to speak of the clear summer sky and that white, fleecy cloud, which might drive some cameraman crazy. And "crossing the wide room slowly"! That sounds very simple, doesn't it?

"Yet, to cross a wide room slowly, trailing draperies, to sniff roses and look at the sky, might take up several hundred feet of film and leave a blank, actionless space at an important point in the story. The screen audience would shuffle its feet, sneeze, cough, change positions, get bored, and lose a great deal of interest in what has happened and what will happen to the rose-sniffing lady. Then everyone would say that the book or the play was faithfully transmitted to the screen; but, after all, was it really a story suitable to the screen?"

Gloria Swanson in a scene from "Sunset Boulevard"

Charlie Chaplin (1934)

He came toward me with a frank, open look—a small, closely knit man who, obviously, had won through to serenity—or at least an appearance of serenity—which, earlier, had not been his. There was in him a fresh vigor and in his eyes a lively sparkle which I had not expected.

One meets actors without searching their facial expressions for the roles they portray on the stage, and without trying to analyze them from these expressions. They have worked facial transformations too many times. So many masks have passed across their features that when we see them in person we expect to see only a blank and empty tablet. And that, too often, is what we find.

But here, for once, was an actor with only a single rôle, and in it he has been seen a hundred times. In this case I looked for no double, no *alter ego*, no simulated rôle, taking the place of the man himself. With Chaplin, on the contrary, it is the individual himself who has, amazingly, concealed himself in the stage character.

"I am a man of the town," he told me. "I was born in the city, I have lived in cities; they suit me and I suit them. In a city, London, I received the impressions of my childhood, tragic and comic. There too I created my first film rôle.

"How did that come about? Sheer chance, of course. A minor director had taken me from the talking stage to play, along with a crowd of others, the rôle of a comic guest in a hotel foyer. I told myself:

" 'You must take clothes that do not fit, a hat that is too small, trousers that are too wide and too long, shoes that are big and awkward.'

"People laughed at the grotesque little figure I made. When I played the rôle a second time, there were some among the spectators who saw that there was something more in this curious figure than met the eye. Soon this tragi-comic little figure had impressed itself upon more people. Then it became famous.

"I was discovered by no critic. I was discovered by the crowd—the crowd from which I myself had come."

Jackie Coogan with Chaplin in the 1921 movie "The Kid."

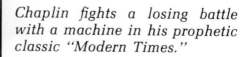

Chaplin fights a losing battle with a machine in his prophetic classic "Modern Times."

27

Greta Garbo and the handsome John Gilbert.

Greta Garbo (1929)

Greta Garbo was once head over heels in love with Jack Gilbert.

At the time, the Garbo-Gilbert romance was played down by the heavily censored Hollywood press. But now it may as well be admitted that this was a red-hot he-man and she-woman love affair.

When Greta began working with the great Gilbert, most glamorous and dynamic of masculine stars, she was still a wide-eyed little onlooker beside the Hollywood scene. But she could talk a little English with her tongue and a whole dictionaryful of universal language with her eyes. With the latter she devoured Gilbert from the beginning. And Jack, who was not hard to get, responded with the hottest love-making in cinema history.

There weren't any "closed sets" for Garbo in those days. She hadn't reached the state where she couldn't work with anybody watching her. So the studio gang used to gather around whenever a love scene was in prospect, and got vicarious thrills that they never forgot.

"Now, Miss Garbo," Director Clarence Brown would announce, after looking at the script, "you say, 'My body burns for love—I want you—only you.' "

Greta would move her lips in silent ecstasy. Her greenish-blue eyes would narrow into heavily lidded slits. Her lips would part hungrily. Her long pale hands would tremble as they found each other behind Jack's neck. Down she would go almost to a reclining position as his stong arms swept around her shoulders and their lips met in one of those kisses.

There were never any retakes on Garbo-Gilbert love scenes—they got them right the first time!

W.C.Fields (1937)

As a juggler with comedy gags and pantomime W. C. Fields traveled all over the world. The characterizations you see today are all pulled out of the storehouse of his amazing memory. Yet his memory is for people, not for facts or lines from a play. Never drilled, as are most youngsters, to study and remember, he has absolutely no ability to learn lines or routine stage business. He was the despair of Broadway managers and Hollywood directors until they discovered that the business and words he improvises are much funnier than the ones he is supposed to learn.

Ten years with the Ziegfeld Follies established him firmly as a leading comic. But between his great renown in New York and his recent success in pictures came one of those low periods so common to actors. "After Flo Ziegfeld died, nobody in New York wanted me," Bill said. "All my savings were in a bank that went flooey, so I thought I'd try my luck at the coast. I was so broke that people were picking up stray pieces of Mr. Fields all over Hollywood Boulevard

"In desperation I went to a studio—no, I won't tell you which—and I made them a proposition. 'I'll write, direct, and act in a two-reel comedy for nothing!' I told them. You don't have to pay me a salary. All I want is for you to finance this first picture. If it goes over, I'll expect you to engage me for others.' Did they listen? Nix. I'll bet their faces are red now!"

One of the more striking poses of W. C. Fields.

Boris Karloff (1941)

Being a bogeyman—like baggage smashing and truck driving—is apt to be a rather exhausting occupation. I know, because I've tried all three. On the whole, I think I would prefer truck driving to house haunting were it not for the fact that my current job is apt to be more remunerative. And, of course, you meet the most interesting werewolves!

Nevertheless the Hollywood horror man runs into numerous occupational hazzards that have

Karloff in his most famous role. He was not Dr. Frankenstein but rather the monster.

nothing to do with the hours of work or the risks run in actual performance.

There is, for example, one's social life to consider. Although Hollywood actors have long since come to realize that their private lives are everyone's concern but their own, they have at least the comfort of knowing that their public is certain to be reasonably well disposed toward them. Not so in my case.

For, no matter how pleasant the company in which I find myself, there is always that awkward moment when newcomers become aware of the fact that the quiet, soft-spoken man in the corner is actually Boris Karloff. (The more horrific my current role, the more I tend to modulate my voice off duty.) Nor are hostesses ever quite sure upon what I feed myself while other guests are sipping their whisky-and-sodas.

As a result, they become convinced that a typical dinner for Karloff should consist of (*a*) one steaming witch's potion, (*b*) one piece of red raw meat ripped from a live and struggling anatomy, (*c*) one soothing bowl of fresh blood. But, whatever the jest with which hostesses try to pass off their uneasiness, I am often aware that they look upon me with about the same degree of trust and confidence as they would upon a cobra de capello!

Acquaintances, asking me to their summer home, fill their medicine cabinets with such niceties as arsenic, old daggers, strychnine, cyanide, and ground glass—somehow feeling that this will make me happy.

Typical of the embarrassment attendant upon my sort of career was an incident that occurred shortly after the filming of Frankenstein. Mrs. Karloff and I had gone up to San Francisco to visit one of her school friends. To our surprise, we found that Frankenstein, which we had not yet seen, was playing across the bay, in Oakland. What could be more natural than to invite our friend to a performance?

I had, of course, seen rushes of the picture, but never a connected version, and as the film progressed I was amazed at the hold it was taking upon the audience. At the same time I couldn't help wondering how my own performance would weather all the build-up.

I was soon to know.

Suddenly, out of the eerie darkness and gloom, there swept on the screen, about eight sizes larger than life itself, the chilling horrendous figure of me as the Monster!

And, just as suddenly, there crashed out over the general stillness the stage whisper of my wife's friend. Covering her eyes, gripping my wife by the shoulder, she screamed:

"Dot, how can you live with *that* creature?"

Burns and Allen   (1938)

There have been teams of funny comedians on the screen and vaudeville stage before Burns and Allen. There are great comedy teams today on stage and screen and air; among others, Laurel and Hardy, Willie and Eugene Howard, Myrt and Marge, Amos 'n' Andy, the Strouds, and, of course, Edgar Bergen and Charlie McCarthy.

But for sheer goofiness there never has been and probably never will be a rival entry to these "nitwits of the network," Burns and Allen.

To Gracie especially go the well earned titles of "America's favorite nitwit," "the no-brains girl," "the dumb Dora of screen and air." Her "dizzy giggle, moronic voice, and gushing inanities" have made her a symbol of all that is moon-struck and pixilated.

"No one thinks my wife's funny," moans her admiring husband. "They think she's just crazy."

"George tells me I have been on the radio for nearly six years now, but whenever I turn on the radio in our house I never get me."

Gracie is apparently in a continual state of bewilderment as to world events. "I've just been reading in the papers," she is quoted as saying, "that the Los Angeles police are hunting for a Chicago gangster. But why should they want one from Chicago? Can't they be satisfied with a home-town boy?"

Their current contract is unique in the history of show business, providing for continuous three-way employment on the screen, on the stage, and on the air.

"The rest," says Mr. Burns, "is history."

"History?" says Mrs. Burns. "That sounds familiar. What is it, Georgie Porgie?"

"Gracie, you know. Napoleon, Hannibal, Caesar—"

"What stations are they on?"

"Quiet, Gracie! Well, Lincoln, then. You must have heard of him."

"Oh, yes; I just heard the other day. And wasn't it too bad?"

The young Birnbaums can hardly believe all that has happened to them since the country became Burns and Allen conscious. Gracie is especially confused.

The great comedy team of Burns & Allen.

30

Armstrong/Teagarden (1948)

Mr. T: Reverend Satchelmouth, tell me, what is your text for today?

Mr. A.: Well, Elder Teabutton, the time has come to talk about that exclusively American art form known as the Blues.

Mr. T.: First time I ever encountered the Blues was back in Vernon, Texas, in short-pants days. I heard somebody sing the song about St. James Infirmary. It moved me like no music ever had before. When did you first hear the Blues, Louis?

Mr. A.: Big Gate, when I was a boy in Storyville I used to hustle "stone" coal after school. That's what we called hard coal. Every evening I would go along my route, hurrying fast as I could, until I got to Pete Lala's cabaret. Then I would stand quietly, hoping I wouldn't be noticed, while I listened to King Oliver's band playing inside.

Mr. T.: No one could ask for a more authentic introduction to the Blues than a course with Professor King Oliver. Too bad all those wonderful Blues specialists were so seldom recorded.

Mr. A.: Many of them never saw a recording studio. But the greatest of them all did make records. That was Bessie Smith, who was properly billed wherever she appeared as "The Empress of the Blues."

Mr. T.: I never heard anyone put so much feeling into the Blues. When she talked about her man, why, there couldn't be any misunderstanding about her heartbreak. Columbia has just reissued a set of records Bessie made in 1929, 1930, and 1933. [Set C-142.] And I'm proud those four 1933 sides are included, because I was in that Bessie Smith band, and believe me, Bessie was inspiring.

Mr. A.: Someone named Benny Goodman played the clarinet that day, too.

Mr. T.: But the Blues didn't pass with Bessie. Today there are youngsters coming up playing and singing a whole mess of Blues.

Mr. A.: Isn't it the truth! There's that Lucky Thompson & His Lucky Seven [Victor.] with a bright new record called Boppin' the Blues. There's a fast-moving teen-age band called Bob Wilbur's Wildcats. I like their Mabel's Dream. [Commodore.] And as far as swinging those Blues is concerned, who's going to do it better than that man with the Kansas City keyboard, Count Basie? I'm fixing to wear out his Brand New Wagon. [Victor.]

Mr. T.: And don't forget Eddie Condon's free-wheeling kind of blues. Eddie was the man who put the Blues on the symphony platform. His latest album expresses his philosophy about the Blues.

Mr. A.: What does he call it, Gate?

Mr. T.: His title is We Called It Music. [Decca.]

Mr. A.: That is the sermon I wanted to preach today.

Mr. T.: Doxology!

Mr. A.: Use all the doors! Use all the doors!

EDITOR'S NOTE: Jazz authorities seldom agree on anything. But there is one basic that all of them seem to accept. That is simply that Louis Armstrong and Jack Teagarden are the greatest living exponents of the Blues. Louis and Jack, united these days in a concert group, have recently made two unusual Blues records. They are The Fifty Fifty Blues and the Jack Armstrong Blues. [Victor.]

Jack Teagarden and Louis Armstrong, are considered two of the greatest jazz men of all time.

Humphrey Bogart (1947)

Humphrey Bogart, a guy with a slight lisp, played tough guys in films, doing it so well that a Bogart cult exists today. This means that art theatres run his pictures and after each performance the faithful get together and talk about them.

Few would have predicted this at the start of Bogey's career. He was born in New York, the son of a well-to-do family, with a mother prominent in various causes. Humphrey drifted into the theatre because a schoolmate was the son of a Broadway producer and the life sounded interesting. He began playing romantic juvenile leads, the sort of good looking boys who bounded onstage carrying a tennis racquet. Bogart did these roles—he was even in something called Cradle Snatchers—until 1929, when real opportunity knocked with Robert E. Sherwood's Petrified Forest. In this, he played Duke Mantee, a hard bitten gangster on the run, from whom a young John Dillinger may have got ideas. Hollywood wanted Leslie Howard, star of the play, to repeat his performance in a movie version. Howard said, "I won't sign unless Bogey is Duke Mantee." Hollywood agreed, the picture was a hit, and Bogey went on to play another gangster in High Sierra.

There was variety in Bogart's roles after that. Sometimes he played a real toughie, at others his rough exterior hid a breaking heart. Once in a while he walked off with the girl, and audiences went home happy. In real life Bogey got Lauren Bacall, a girl just out of high school who played opposite him in To Have and Have Not. He also starred in Dead End, Black Legion, North Atlantic, Maltese Falcon, Treasure of Sierra Madre, African Queen, and other pictures. Probably he's best remembered for Casablanca, with its "Play it again, Sam."

Bogey was such an effortless actor that he just seemed to be playing himself. There's some truth there, for he liked to drink and engaged in headlined sparring matches with Mayo Methot, his first wife. But the real Bogey was an honest, intelligent guy who hated sham. With friends he could be sentimental and generous, and he loved kids and animals. For more, ask that Bogart cult.

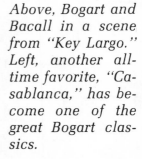

Above, Bogart and Bacall in a scene from "Key Largo." Left, another all-time favorite, "Casablanca," has become one of the great Bogart classics.

Joan Crawford (1938)

Joan Crawford is wearing white tailored shorts and a beige pull-over costing as much as the average evening gown. Her physical trainer—paid by the star to keep her slim hips slim—has just played three hard sets with her. He calls goodby as she runs past her emerald swimming pool, glittering in the California sun, and disappears inside her expensive home.

In the mirrored dressing room the hairdresser waits. As expert fingers arrange the crisp chestnut curls, Joan reads the more important fan mail, sent from the studio by the secretary assigned to her.

A maid appears at the dressing-room door, asking madame to put her final approval on the menu for the dinner party tonight—clear soup, stuffed lobster, duck and wild rice, endive-and-chive salad, hot cherries in ice ring—white wine with the fish, champagne with the fowl, coffee, and Napoleon brandy.

"O.K.," says Joan.

The butler knocks softly. Will madame select the program for tonight's film showing? Joan checks from the paper he hands her on a silver tray—a newsreel, a Mickey Mouse comedy, an unreleased feature. These will unfold after dinner as she and her guests sit in her private theater beyond the swimming pool.

Her coiffeur rolls the chromium-plated hair dryer forward and adjusts it over Joan's curls. While her nails are being manicured the star picks up a script her supervisor has asked her to consider and wonders what she will wear tonight.

The choice is a shimmering blue satin gown. It will look well with her diamond-and-star-sapphire bracelet, the diamond-and-star-sapphire clip, the sapphire ring.

One last look in the maze of mirrors tells her she is perfect, the dress revealing every curve of a lovely body, her hair combed out to frame a vivid, unreal, beautiful face. On her dressing table is a nosegay of lilies of the valley and pale pink roses. These she holds in one carmine-tipped hand. She walks down the white-carpeted stairs, pausing for a moment on the landing. Her husband, Franchot Tone, goes to her, touching the hand free of flowers.

"How nice you look, Joan," he says.

Joan Crawford, million-dollar-contract box-office star, has arrived in her own drawing room.

Joan Crawford with a young Melvyn Douglas.

Howdy Doody

Anyone who recalls the early days of TV knows Howdy Doody, the variety puppet show beloved of every moppet (young or old) who ever watched the show about the knee-high puppet and his sidekick and alter ego, Bob Smith, who started the program on the NBC network late in 1947.

Buffalo Bob, Howdy and the cast wave hello.

Do you remember Buffalo Bob and the Peanut Gallery?

Howdy Doody's real life began in Buffalo in the early part of the decade. Bob Smith, then presiding over a chatter-and-record show on a local radio station decided to add a little more fun to the broadcasts by introducing a drawling, oafish voice (his own, in higher register) and named his character Elmer. In 1947, Bob moved to New York to do an early morning children's program on WNBC. Suddenly he was assigned to a Saturday morning children's program. It was a quiz show with a Western format called Triple B Ranch. To amuse his listeners Bob revived his old pal Elmer. Because Elmer always started out with the words "Howdy Doody, kids," the kids were soon calling him Howdy Doody. So Howdy Doody was born.

Next the children were demanding to see more of Howdy Doody, and a television show was the natural result. As a weekly half-hour program the show made its debut and within several months was such a hit that it got three half-hour periods a week. Then it went on a five-day schedule.

The popular show was peopled by Bob Smith and the fanciful characters Clarabelle, Mr. Bluster, Dilly Dally, the Flub-a-Dub, and a clown who never spoke. The gal who manipulated Howdy Doody was Rhoda Mann, called Howdy Doody's Mama by those who knew about her.

Howdy Doody ran for thirteen long years, with its theme song "Howdy Doody Time" whistled all over the country.

Ed Sullivan

Mimics make fun of Ed Sullivan. His dead-pan, wooden gestures, and that atonal voice. But you can't belittle Ed's career. He stayed in television longer than any of the pioneers like Milton Berle, Sid Caesar, and Dave Garroway. More than that, he entertained millions once a week.

Ed is the pride of Port Chester, N.Y., and grew up with dual interests. He liked the newspaper game and wanted to be a reporter. But he loved show biz, though at the time he didn't seem to have the talent for it. He got his job as a reporter and then a columnist for the New York Daily News, but all the time kept alive that burning interest in show biz. Ed emceed talent shows, and ran a famous celebrity interviewing radio show over CBS. When television dawned, he dipped into his memory bag and pulled out the formula of an outmoded entertainment called vaudeville. It was a varying series of acts just strung together for an evening's entertainment.

Ed improved on the old days by becoming the emcee who introduced each TV act and gave a few words of explanation. When the act was over, the girls kissed him and guys warmly shook his hand. Ed said a few more words, and the next act was on. As simple and as inspired as that!

All good things come to an end and the Ed Sullivan show, which had its own Broadway theatre, seems to be gone. But maybe it's only a hiatus. Ed still does his column and works on TV specials. Friends say he likes to talk about the past. No wonder—he's had a good one.

Ed tries a trick shot with Red Skelton's help.

Ed Sullivan, television's original Master of Ceremonies.

Bing Crosby

Bing Crosby hit the airwaves as a crooner—remember that word? This was the beginning of the Depression, and besides being a newstyle singer Bing seemed like a heartening example of the boy next door making good at a time of national stress. With Kate Smith, Russ Columbo, Perry Como, and Amos' n' Andy, Bing kept the country enlivened through some very dark days.

At the same time, he was appearing in movies like The Big Broadcast with such radio luminaries as the Boswell Sisters, Mills Brothers, Burns and Allen, and Street Singer Arthur Tracy. From then on he alternated between films and radio, showing amazing versatility in each. In radio, his best program was perhaps the Kraft Music Hall, a relaxed (it had to be, with Bing) hour of music and patter with Jerry Colonna, Bob Burns, Bob Hope, and the John Scott Trotter Orchestra. Still, he kept on making movies—more, it seems, than you can count. Most popular were the Road to —— series, with Bob Hope and Dotty Lamour. But who can forget his serious acting roles like Going My Way and Country Girl?

Some call Bing the most popular singer of the Twentieth Century, pointing to White Christmas and other songs as proof. Others claim Francis Albert Sinatra has grabbed the honor. But however Bing rates, he's always been tops and, as someone says, thanks for the memory.

Bing Crosby and Bob Hope teamed up to make some of the funniest movies of all time.

Bing Crosby, Danny Kaye and Vera-Ellen sing and dance in one of all the all-time popular holiday musicals, "White Christmas." The musical score for this movie was written by Irving Berlin.

Frank Sinatra

Frank Sinatra rose from high school dropout, to darling of the bobby-sox generation, to a grown man in his mid-fifties with a private jet plane and an envious lifestyle.

His outstanding success only points up the versatility of today's top entertainers, who move blithely from one medium to another. The great Al Jolson was a sensation in the first talking movie, but then lost all his popularity because he couldn't act. Bing Crosby, however, can play a gentle Irish priest in Going My Way, and Sinatra an Academy Award performance in From Here to Eternity or a dope addict in Man with the Golden Arm.

Sinatra's success seems easy when you read about it, but the fellow who didn't like school books worked hard and cleverly along the way. In his days with the Tommy Dorsey orchestra, he practiced breath control to make his voice hold notes like Dorsey's trombone. From then on his musical road was up. In 1944, he turned to movie musicals and made top ones like Anchors Aweigh, On the Town, and Pal Joey. Still, his dramatic roles were tops with the public—until his one-man TV shows.

The world knows about Sinatra's low boiling point, his generosity, his restlessness, his girls, and his busted marriages. He's sung just about every important song over the last thirty years, and has been particularly lucky with his own hit songs. One of them is I Did It My Way. You can say that again about Frank Sinatra. He did it his way.

Frank Sinatra, one of the greatest all around entertainers, charmed 3 generations of Americans.

A scene from "A Hole in the Head" starred Frank with Edward G. Robinson.

Jean Harlow

Jean Harlow was the screen's first Platinum Blonde. Publicity called her the Blonde Bombshell. For those who don't remember, she was the Marilyn Monroe of her day. Jean was a Sex Symbol (she never wore a bra, even then) who made her first appearance during the late Twenties in Howard Hughes' Hells' Angels. From then on her films got naughtier and you can say that more than any other star Jean was responsible for the morality code adopted by movie companies. She was making a picture called Born to Be Kissed when the Code went into effect; the title was hastily changed to 100% Pure. After the sexy roles Jean turned out to be a girl with a gift for tough-gal comedy. She was excellent in Dinner at Eight and other super productions, but her top grosses came from Red Dust, Hold Your Man and the others with leading man Clark Gable.

Was she happy with all this? Unfortunately not. Jean complained loudly to interviewers about the long hours and hard work of picture making. Her troubles went deeper than that. She was an ill-starred girl who seemed to have everything, including a mansion high in the hills with a swimming pool. But to her it was nothing; she felt empty inside. One of her husbands killed himself in a blast of ugly publicity. Her next mate was wrong for her. In 1934, at the peak of her career, Jean herself died, chiefly because she lacked interest in living. Her pictures were shown again after her death and the morbid flocked to see them again.

Jean Harlow and Clark Gable followed Gilbert and Garbo as the screen's torrid lovers.

38

Marilyn Monroe

You could write a magazine article, or maybe a book, about the similarities between Jean Harlow and Marilyn Monroe, our own recent Sex Symbol. For one thing, they were both discovered by the same guy. He was Ben Lyon, debonair actor turned casting genius. Seeing Marilyn, he shouted ecstatically, "It's Jean Harlow all over again!"

In many ways, it was. Marilyn lived glamorously (or so it seemed to us) but couldn't seem to find herself amidst the glitter of stardom. She thought faster than Jean Harlow and said things that sounded dumb but really were smart. After she had posed nude for a calendar a reviewer asked, "Didn't you wear *anything?*" "Oh, yes," she answered, "I had the radio on." As with Harlow, there was outrage about the morality of some of her pictures. "The trouble is that they worry whether a girl has cleavage," she said. "They ought to worry if she hasn't any." Again she told a reporter, "Sex is part of nature, and I go along with nature."

The woes of Sex Symbol Marilyn had roots in problems that concern us all—foster homes, sudden success, mixed-up marriages. She never had a normal home life, and the three men she married didn't seem able to make up for it. Yet her performances showed none of this. Like Harlow, she had a glorious gift for light comedy, along with a silky-soft voice for delivery. She could act too, and proved it in pictures like Niagara. Yet she was best in light comedies like Gentlemen Prefer Blondes and Seven Year Itch. Let's cherish her that way.

Like Jean Harlow, Marilyn Monroe was a clever comedienne, as she proves in scene from the movie "Some Like It Hot."

SPORTS AND SPORTS HEROES

The Twenties are hailed as the Golden Age of Sports and no one has yet risen to say it ain't so. Babe Ruth, Jack Dempsey, Bobby Jones, tennis-player Bill Tilden, Channel-swimmer Gertrude Ederle, and others were at the height of their spectacular careers.

Jack Dempsey, the so-called Manassa Mauler, was probably the most ferocious prizefighter the game has ever known. He won the heavyweight title from lumbering Jess Willard in 1919, and went on to beat the Gorgeous Georges Carpentier of France and tough Tom Gibbons. On a hot night in 1923, he was propelled out of the ring in the first round by the mighty fist of Luis Angel Firpo, known as the Wild Bull of the Pampas. Here, in his own terse words, Jack tells what he did to finish that fabled fight.

Rough-edged Babe Ruth was the most picturesque player in baseball history. Starting out as a pitcher, he switched to the outfield and became the game's foremost home run hitter, who used to point to the spot in the bleachers where his record-breaking smashes would land. Babe was a tobacco-chewing graduate of an orphanage in Baltimore, and had managed to skip the pleasures of education. One day a college-bred fellow named Lou Gehrig became a Yankee, and began his own series of home runs. Newspapers tried to build up a rivalry between these two superstars, but Gehrig says the opposite was true. The Babe was friendly to him and the two formed a friendship rare in baseball. Here Lou tells how he felt about his immortal teammate.

No one ever played golf like Robert Tyre Jones, Jr., of Atlanta, known as "Bobby" to sports fans of the twenties. You name the tournament, he won it. Yet even to this incredible player, the tournaments were a strain, as you see here.

Am I Jealous of Babe Ruth?

by Lou Gehrig

Lou Gehrig wrote this article in 1933, at the height of his fame. But the Babe had been callously traded by the Yankees and quit baseball.

When a fighter makes good, newspapers always relate, "He is good to his mother." Many people laugh. The phrase has become a bromide. The sports writers continually remind me that Babe Ruth is my inspiration. But he isn't. He's my pal, and he has been my adviser. But my mother is my inspiration, my sweetheart, my manager, my all. Around her revolve all of my activities.

My tale is unusual, at least. Let me tell it to you.

The scene was Sportsman's Park, St. Louis; the occasion, the final game of the 1928 World Series between the Yankees and Cardinals; the situation:

Ruth had just hit his third home run of the game, a tremendous performance in more ways than one. Only an inning or two before, he had warned the St. Louis fans by pantomime and word of mouth that he would hit three home runs before the day was done!

He now was pedaling his way around third base and into the plate, while the stands rocked and roared. A moment later, the demonstration having settled down to a barely audible hum, Willie Sherdel, Cardinal left-hander at the time, took his place on the rubber, wound up—and I hit the first ball pitched for a home run into the right-field bleachers!

So much for Scene Number One.

Number Two was Wrigley Field, Chicago, during the third game of the 1932 World's Series between the Yankees and Cubs. Except for the change of date, opponent, and city, the situation was the same. Ruth, heckled by the Cubs from the bench, had pointed to the farthest section of the centerfield bleachers with his index finger to show what he meant to do. And then he did it!

Probably no gesture in all the history of baseball was the equal of this, and as he ambled around the bases in that peculiar sidling run of his, the place was a madhouse. It was Ruth's second home run of the game and his third of the series.

Finally everything settled down again. The

41

Cubs went back to their positions, Charley Root resumed his place on the rubber, wound up—and I hit the first ball pitched for a home run into the right-field bleachers!

I was probably the most surprised man in the park on both occasions. I didn't swing hard. I wasn't trying to imitate Ruth, but merely to meet the ball, to get one safe. And I was secretly pleased when the reporters missed the remarkable coincidence of those two homers of mine, because they're always saying that Babe is my inspiration, my guiding spirit; that without him I might have been just another ball player, probably no worse than the average, certainly no better. And that's only partly true.

The Babe and I are not competitors—never have been. We haven't fought each other; we've fought together for the good of both and the ball club, so that when one hits a home run the other is able to say to himself with satisfaction:

"That's one for us."

The Babe himself outlined this idea in a talk we had six or seven years ago, when it became apparent that I had something of a career before me as a slugger. Anyhow, he came up to me one day and began to get confidential—something like this:

"Say, young fellow"—I was always "young fellow" to him in those days—"there's a lot of fun in this game, but the money's the thing we're after. It's over there"—pointing—"back of those fences. All we have to do is go get it! The more balls we hit over the wall, the more World's Series we'll figure in. That's where the money is. Suppose we forget each other and remember that."

I have never forgotten it and I'm certain that he still feels the same way, too. In any case, there never was a question of jealousy between us, even when I ran well ahead of him for most of the 1927 season.

I went to the High School of Commerce, playing baseball and football, and working through the summer months. In my fourth year I had several college scholarships offered to me but didn't give the matter a thought. After all, I wasn't going to college. I was going to work. So what good was a scholarship?

"You're to be a civil engineer," my mother said firmly. "I've always wanted that for you. Now you're going to have it."

That fall found me up at Columbia University, waiting on the table, trying to study, and playing a little baseball and football in between. For two years there I lived like a time clock. Up at six thirty in the morning and over to the dining hall to set the tables; busy as a fool there until eight fifty, when I dropped everything and hustled across the campus to classes. Then football or baseball in the late afternoon, depending on the season, after which I jumped out of my uniform, under a shower, into my clothes, and finally on to the street. The next stop was the dining hall again, where I was busy waiting on table and washing dishes until nine at night—when, outside of a few hours for study, I had the rest of the time to myself.

I guess I didn't have much time for study, in fact, but I was reasonably happy. That is, for a while. My father had lost a lot of time from work owing to illness, and we were having a tough time meeting our bills.

Finally my mother was taken ill with double pneumonia—and the bottom fell out of my college career! We were five months behind in the rent and I knew that something had to be done. I had received several major-league offers from the Yankees and Senators but had dismissed them. I was to be a civil engineer. But now I signed with the Yanks. Very well do I remember my introduction to Ruth. He always has the first locker near the door at the Yankee Stadium, and he was getting into his uniform when they brought me in and introduced us. I mumbled something.

"We Ain't So Bad"

"Hello, young fellow," he boomed in that hearty natural way of his. "Hope you like us. We ain't so bad and we ain't so good, but we strike a fair average. Hope you stick with us."

I was out with Hartford before the end of the season. But the die had been cast. Not only did I have a good year up there, but the fairness and friendliness of the ball field had gotten into my blood and warmed my heart to it.

Tris Speaker had been a boyhood idol. And the first time we passed each other on the diamond, he smiled and nodded to me. I lived in a glow for days after that. Then we went from Cleveland to Chicago.

"Hello, Columbia!" I looked up to find Eddie Collins, himself a football and baseball man at

Columbia in the old days. We had a great visit together, talking it over.

I hung on through the following season, and then came my chance early in 1925 and I've never been out of the line-up since. I was still awed by Ruth and kept away from him as much as possible. But he seemed to like me and made a point of talking to me on the bench between innings and sitting with me on road trips, and after awhile my shyness wore off and I got to know him for what he was and is. He's just one of the boys, unaffected by all the attention he's got and demanding no consideration that any other player on the club doesn't receive.

By the time I had enough money to go back to college it was too late. I was part of baseball and baseball was a very big part of me.

However, I went out that first winter and got a job with the electric company—just in case! I was still pretty awkward around first base. I guess I am yet.

Off the ball grounds I'm just a plain comfort-loving citizen who likes to go to bed early and take life at a slow pace. I smoke a little, drink a little beer, like fishing and ice skating, and just recently I've begun to go for golf.

When I broke into the regular line-up, Walter Johnson was just about getting through. But you couldn't prove it by what he showed me. He knew all the answers by that time and his fast one was still a puff of wind as it went by. Grove and Earnshaw and Ferrell and a lot of others came on later, but I got one break out of it. I never had to hit against Herb Pennock when he was at the top. There was a left-hander. Boy, I salute him! He had everything. So did Alexander, a tricky old bird with perfect coördination and without nerves. You never knew what he was going to do, and while you were still trying to guess he did it!

Surprise for Tony

I always thought that Tony Lazzeri hadn't been quite ready for that last strike Alexander pitched to him, practically deciding the 1926 series in favor of the Cardinals. The bases were filled, two were out, and it looked as though we were due, particularly when Haines had to leave the game with a torn finger nail. He turned the pitching job over to Alexander.

He took plenty of time coming across the

The All Stars, Waite Hoyt, Babe Ruth and Lou Gehrig.

43

field from the bull pen. Having stalled long enough to get Tony anxious, Alexander changed his routine swiftly. Still outwardly careless, he grabbed the ball and took his five warm-up pitches as fast as O'Farrell, the catcher, could get the ball back. Then, without a glance at anybody, he began pitching to Lazzeri just as he always pitched, rapidly and with no attempt to steady himself. The effect he always gave on the mound was of a pitcher working in batting practice.

Finally the count got to three and two, and it seemed that even the apparently indifferent Alexander must take time, at a moment as critical as this, to kind of stiffen himself for the show-down. But he didn't. Just as though it were a ten-cent ball game, he took that quick little wind-up of his and broke a low-curve ball down around the knees, and Tony missed it. We were one run behind at the time and never caught up. I always thought that maybe Tony was a little surprised by the fact that the ball had left Alexander's hand so soon.

The Babe vs. the Cubs

Anyhow, it stands to reason that major-league pitchers are just as good as the hitters or they wouldn't be up there. Even that exhibition of English cricketing we seemed to be doing in the last World's Series was hardly a normal outburst. Out hitters just weren't that good and the Cub pitchers just couldn't have been that bad. I think they became panicky when, after all their riding and chattering, we just smiled quietly and busted the next one.

Ruth began it. I might add that he also finished it. But at the time I don't think he meant anything in particular, except that he was a little burned up when he heard that Mark Koenig, who had once been with our club, had been cut in for only a half share of the receipts by the Cubs. He had joined the club late in the season, true enough, but even so, he had practically won the pennant for them.

So, without thinking much about anything, Ruth cupped his hands and hollered at Koenig from the bench during the practice before the first game:

"Hey, Mark! You'd better get four for four today or they'll cut you to a quarter share."

By "four for four" he meant a perfect average at the plate, with four hits in four times

up. If the Cubs had let that ride, the matter would have been dropped. But they opened up on the Babe with a storm of abuse which got pretty personal as the series wore on, and I guess we weren't so far behind. However, we kept our minds on our business and maybe the Cubs didn't—or else you can say that we can take it and the Cubs can't. They played like a high-school team in that first game, making mistakes I didn't think were possible on a major-league field.

The funny thing was that the worse they got the louder they chattered, which made them a little comical. Ruth was "yellow," he was "a big dog," etc., and all the time he was handling their pitchers as though they were a lot of cricket bowlers.

We won the first two games in a romp and then headed for Chicago, with the Yanks still hitting and the Cubs still yelping. They must have felt pretty good about getting home, because they opened up from the bench with a tirade that made their New York performance seem pale by comparison.

When Ruth came to bat in one of the early innings, they were all set to give him a blast that would blow his ears back. The big fellow glanced over at them casually, and then, just as though it didn't really matter after all, he pointed to the farthest point of the outfield fence in dead centerfield and said:

"That's where I'm going to hit it this time."

The Cubs howled in derision and their coach stood up in front of the dugout to lead the jeers. Charley Root, the pitcher, then burned one across for a strike and Ruth "took it." That is, he didn't swing. It looked like a good ball to hit, but apparently that wasn't his plan.

As the umpire called the strike, the Cubs leaped up in a frenzy. But all Ruth did was to solemnly raise one finger as though he were keeping score for them. A few moments later Root got another one across and the Cubs went crazy again. But the Babe didn't even glance at the ball as it went by. He just kept his position at the plate with his legs spread a little, took his left hand off the bat, and raised two fingers. Then he nodded significantly toward the centerfield bleachers.

The rest is history. Everybody knows that on the next ball pitched he hit one on a line right where he said he would. He had done the unbelievable. He had called his shot with an almost impossible home run into an almost impossible spot. That finished the Cubs. They didn't even lift their heads when I hit the next ball pitched for a home run that nipped the cord on the flagpole in rightfield as it went by. In fact, I doubt whether my hit attracted much attention anywhere, and for easons cited early in this story, I'm glad it was so.

When we got back to New York we found the town hailing us as "the greatest of all Yankee teams." All I can say to that is we are better than some people seem to think and not so good as the 1927 club, which to my mind was far and away the best club I've seen

When my number is up I'll even manage a club in the minor leagues just to stay in the game, but I don't intend to go to the minors as a player. It wouldn't be enjoyable and I'd only be taking another man's job that I don't need. For the depression didn't get me, as it got so many of my friends, and I'm financially safe now.

So life with the Gehrigs is a pretty fine thing, perhaps a little dull for some tastes. but perfect for a family that asks only to live amiably, quietly, and with contentment. Maybe we're missing something, but I can't help thinking that people who see life as though from a train window must be missing something too. They're going too fast to get anything but a fleeting glimpse of what it's all about.

Awaiting his turn at bat, Gehrig greets Babe as he reaches home after hitting another out of the park.

Goodbye to Golf

by Bobby Jones

The world champion of golf tells of his career from 1927 to 1930 and why he is quitting the game. O. B. Keeler, an Atlanta sports writer, captured the spirit of competition at Winged Foot and Pebble Beach in the 1929 season.

It seems the hardest thing in major golf competion is to win the United States open championship and then come back and win the national amateur. In 1929 I had my third shot at this record, established by Chick Evans in 1916, and accomplished my most noteworthy bust in the endeavor. On the face of it, the problem doesn't look so tough. You accumulate a lot of prestige winning the national open. Everybody then expects you to take the amateur, "in your stride," they all say. I had my first chance in 1923, after winning the open at Inwood, and my "stride" at Flossmoor was more in the nature of a stumble. I lost in the second round to Max Marston, though I should say for Max that he was playing some remarkable golf and I didn't have to do a lot of stumbling to lose a match in which Max was 5 under par for the last nineteen holes. I worked around to the same opening again in 1926, when I had won both the British and the American open titles. This time, at Baltusrol, everybody seemed especially sure I was going to make the grade. And I did get to the very last round, where George Von Elm outplayed me conclusively in a corking match.

I led off, in the latter part of June, 1929, by gaining the American open at Winged Foot—once more with a play-off—and as I had no other serious golf that season except the national amateur at Pebble Beach, everything looked as propitious as possible.

So I went all the way out to California and put on the prize bust of my career, losing in the first round to Johnny Goodman.

I really felt pretty confident of matching Chick's record when I went to Pebble Beach. I had scraped through at Winged Foot by the grace of God, you might say; and the amateur didn't look as drastic as usual, though you never can regard it as a push-over. I suppose golf is different from most other individual competitions. In boxing, for example, I can understand a competitor feeling really confident when he knows he is "right." He has only one opponent, and in boxing, as in tennis, if he is on his game and happens to be a shade better than the other fellow, why, he doesn't let the other fellow play *his* game.

But in golf, all you can do is to play your own game. You can't do anything to keep the other fellow from holing explosion shots out of bunkers or sticking a long iron up against the flag, or running down a forty-foot putt. In the amateur, there is always an excellent chance that one of your five opponents may be extremely hot; and in the open—well, you are up against 150 in that tournament, all at once, and there's no telling how many may be running a temperature.

Thus golf is different from most other individual competitive games, and I can say honestly that I never went into any major competition in a confident frame of mind. Sometimes I felt less confident than others—that's the difference.

But having scraped through the American open, I did feel that I had a better chance than usual at Pebble Beach. We will come to that later.

The national open of 1929, over Mr. Tillinghast's pet course, Winged Foot, found me playing pretty decently in practice; well enough indeed, so that I took a day off on Wednesday and rested instead of playing one or two more rounds before the show started.

Winged Foot, I should say, is preeminently a second-shot course, like Oakmont and in contradistinction to Olympia Fields, at which latter a long and accurate drive is needed if you are going to score.

Winged Foot is not a severe course from the tee. But no matter how well you are driving, the design is such that your second shots at the longer holes must be extremely accurate and kept well under control. The greens are small and the trapping is beautiful—as long as you manage to stay out of its clutches. There is no comforting fringe of grass about the edges to save your ball from trickling off into a bunker on a fairly good shot. The rims of those bunkers are smooth as a billiard ball, and when you see your shot easing over toward one you'd as well haul out the trusty niblick and hope it will be trusty.

One feature of Winged Foot favored me a lot. There were no really short holes. I had lost a lot of shots in previous championships to competitors who were better with the pitching clubs than I, and there were plenty of them at that time. The boys were accustomed to canning deuces against me at these cunning little mashie-niblick holes, while I was working for 3s and picking up an occasional 4—or 5. I never seemed to collect many 2s in the big tournaments. After Winged Foot, when I had played in ten United States open championships—thus having had opportunities for 2s in forty rounds, or at 160 par-3 holes—Innis Brown looked up the record and discovered that I had acquired precisely five 2s.

This certainly is pretty sour in 160 chances. Johnny Farrell, for example, shot three deuces at me in the thirty-six holes of our play-off the previous year. I had none against him, and only one in the preceding competition, of seventy-two holes—and that was at the eighth hole, a good long spoon shot.

At Winged Foot, however, the four one-shot holes measured for the tournament 225 yards, 180 yards, 200 yards, and 230 yards; not a pitch-shotter in the round. And I figured that I'd have a rather better chance against the pitching experts on a course innocent of that type of hole. As it turned out, and for the first time in years, I played the one-shotters about as well as anybody—excepting the first one, of 225 yards—and it was at a couple of medium-length two-shotters that I was so near to spilling the beans in the last round.

My final practice was in a little match with Gene Sarazen against Leo Diegel and Bill Mehlhorn, and I did a 71 with a couple of mistakes and some good putting in it. Leo said he never had seen me hitting the ball so well, and I never had seen Sarazen hitting the ball worse. I think he was as bad as 80. This goes to show how little pre-tournament form may count in the competition, for Gene came on his game suddenly and was in the race right up to the wire, finishing two strokes back of the lead, while Neal McIntyre, with a 69 in his last practice round, used 166 strokes in his first two rounds and was out of the tournament.

Keep Hitting the Ball

I started the show with a ghastly exhibition on the first and third holes. At the first, a long par 4, I was trapped with my second, barely out with the third, and then took three putts for a wretched 6. I nearly holed a six-foot putt for a birdie 3 at the second, taking a par 4 somewhat grudgingly, and missed the green at the 225-yard third. The ball was in a bunker and my blast was soft. I finally reached the green in 3, took two putts, and the 5 cost me two more stokes to par; I was 4 strokes in the

hole as I stood on the fourth tee of the first round. And yet it turned out to be the first round in an American open in which I broke 70.

You can't tell about golf. The best you can do is to follow the example of the Old Master, Harry Vardon. Early in his career, Harry learned one thing well: whatever happened, the only thing to do was to *keep on hitting the ball*.

Sometimes it will suddenly start rolling for you.

As that 120-foot putt at the long fifth hole at St. Andrews, in the first round of the *British* open of 1927, started me on the way to a 68, so the fifth hole at Winged Foot gave me a boost.

This hole is a par 5, of 514 yards, and they are pretty long yards. I had a really big drive there and used a spoon for the second, reaching the green, forty feet from the stick. When that putt disappeared for an eagle 3, I felt for the first time that I might have a good round coming up.

I managed par the rest of the nine and was 38, two strokes over the card. Then one of those funny strings of 3s came along.

I had five of them in a row, one an eagle at the 497-yard twelfth, where a big drive and a No. 3 iron left me twenty feet from the flag and the putt went down. I was bunkered at the thirteenth, a one-shotter of 230 yards, but a niblick blast left the ball a yard from the hold and I had another 3. The last one came at the fourteenth, a hold of 376 yards.

Here I made the best shot of the round, after a badly pulled drive to the deep rough. It was a hacking sort of shot with a spade; the ball stopped five yards from the flag, and I holed the putt. Then I went 4-4-4-4 the rest of the way, for a 31 on the nine, and a card of 69—my best thus far in the United States open.

This was not by any means the best round of the tournament, however. Playing in a hard rain on the second day, which cost me a very hard 75, George Von Elm turned in a card of 70; perhaps the finest round ever played in the American open. And Tommy Armour, under the same conditions, did a 71. Some of the boys, starting early, missed the rain, and Sarazen, with 71, and Al Espinosa, with 72, went into a tie for first place, while Densmore

Bobby Jones was the wonder man of golf in the Roaring Twenties.

Even in Scotland crowds came to watch Bobby Jones.

Shute, with 71, came up into a tie with me. The leading pair were 142 at the halfway post; Shute and I were next with 144; and Armour was a stroke back of us, at 145. It was a real dogfight.

Now, to my way of thinking, I had the most favorable position possible at this stage. It is a terrible strain, leading the chase. You feel like a hunted animal—at least I do—with the pack in full cry behind. You can't help trying to be careful; at any rate I can't. The same trouble seemed to affect the leaders in the third round, next morning, and Sarazen, with a 76, and Espinosa, with 77, dropped back.

Rain Slows the Course

The rain of the previous day had slowed the course, and I felt more secure shooting for the greens. When I worked around with a 71 I was back in the lead. Shute and Armour each had 76, and the scores of the leaders, starting the fourth round, were:

Jones, 69-75-71—215.
Sarazen, 71-71-76—218.
Espinosa, 70-72-77—219.
Shute, 73-71-76—221.

Now I was in the rôle of the fox, and it was only because the pack faltered that I finally reached cover in a tie with Al Espinosa. For in the last round I collapsed with a couple of terrible 7s just when it seemed that everything was all right.

Through the seventh hold, where I barely missed a birdie 2, I had par left for a 36 on the first nine and a commanding lead. Espinosa had gone out in 36, but had run into a dreadful 8 at the twelfth hole, and Sarazen had taken 41 to the turn. I had heard enough of this along the grapevine to feel that a score of 36-36 would win for me by plenty of strokes; and that was what I had in mind as I stood on the eighth tee.

I aimed the drive purposely to the right, wheeling it up into a cross wind over an angle of trees, to cut down the length of the second shot. The drive came off properly enough. But the long pitch, held up too much into the wind, bounded into a deep bunker at the right-front of the green. My first recovery, a controlled explosion, was not controlled enough, and the ball trickled over into another deep bunker beyond the flag. My next blast blew it back in-

to the original trap; I was barely out with the next effort, and two putts made it a 7 for that hole, and left me with a birdie 4 to get out in 38—and a horrid apprehension of any more experiences in bunkers.

Still, with the birdie 4 at the ninth, I was out in 38, and when I was past the long twelfth in 4-4-5 I was leading Espinosa six strokes, with six holes to play. What could be safer?

Now see what golf can do to you.

After that complete collapse at the twelfth, Espinosa, suddenly relieved of all strain, played with incredible brilliance and with four 4s and a couple of 3s finished with a 75 and a total of 294. And this picked up every one of the six strokes by which I had led him.

At the thirteenth hole, par 3, of 230 yards, I pulled a driving iron on to the remains of a large pile of topsoil used for dressing the greens, and was permitted to drop off without penalty, under the upkeep clause of Rule 11. There was a lot of comment about it at the time, but of course the ruling was correct. I lost a stroke there, with a 4; got my 4 at the fourteenth, and then sliced a miserable drive from the fifteenth tee, back of some trees, and had to pitch out short of a ditch and not at all in the direction of the green. I pussyfooted the pitch and the ball stopped in a hanging lie, from which I fired my third over the green into grass knee-deep; was short from the hay with my fourth, on in 5, and took two putts for another 7.

That was calamitous enough. But I still had 4-4-4 to go ahead of Espinosa, who had finished. That was enough to think of, without Denny Shute, who I heard was playing fine golf behind me.

I Missed the Putt

The sixteenth is a par 5, but with the wind I reached it comfortably enough with a drive and iron, twenty feet from the pin. And my first putt was five feet short. I missed the next, and took a 5.

This left 4-4 to tie Espinosa, and after one of the 4s I pulled my pitch for the last green into a bunker from which I chipped badly, and had to hole a twelve-foot putt for the 4. I suppose that was the most important shot of my life. It saved me from going up to 80, a score I never had reached in an American open; but mostly it gave me a tie, and spared me the possible consequences of throwing away a six-stroke lead in the same number of holes.

Shute came on with a good chance to beat us both, but drew three 5s in the last four holes and was tied with Sarazen at 296, Espinosa and I having 294.

I was so relieved by this escape, which I did not deserve, that I went out next day and played my best golf of the week in the play-off. Espinosa was plainly stale, and I won rather easily with scores of 72-69—141.

The California trip to the national amateur was a brilliant and happy affair socially, and I think I played the best golf of my career in the exhibition matches and practice rounds on wonderful courses at Los Angeles and Del Monte. Sometimes I think I shot my tournament in those practice rounds, in one of which I set a course record of 67 at Pebble Beach.

The gallery in practice rounds has become a problem for the player it elects to follow. There really is no such thing as "practice" for him. You can't help putting out, with several thousand following you; and you are more than

Harrison Johnston, top, who captured the cup which Jones passed up at Pebble Beach. Max Marston, center, the Philadelphia amateur, who was Bobby's stumbling block at Flossmoor in 1923. Below, Jones putting on the eighteenth green, Winged Foot, Mamaroneck, N.Y.—1929.

51

likely to go stale. I think that some day—I hope soon—the United States Golf Association will bar spectators from rounds before the tournament for the sake of the competitors. You can't help trying to give them a show and that takes it out of you. In the 67 at Pebble Beach, after starting 5-6-5, I got going at the short fifth and for the next nine holes I had 28 strokes. I was playing rather too well in the rehearsals.

Anyway, I had enough golf left to tie at 145 with Gen Homans for first place in the medal rounds, and then came the match play, in which, for the first time, I was knocked off in the first round.

Johnny Goodman of Omaha was the villain in the plot from my point of view. For some reason I was more nervous than usual before that match. I'm always nervous, and usually I play better the more nervous I am. But this time it worked the other way—at the first two holes, at least. I started with very bad golf—a 5 and a 6—and lost both of them. Johnny then holed a good putt for a birdie 3 at the next, and took that one on its merits. I was 3 down in the first three holes of a short match.

I picked up the fourth with a birdie 3; we halved the short fifth; and I won the long sixth with a birdie 4, and was only 1 down. I tried to get that one back at once, overran a twenty-foot putt for a 2 at the short seventh, missed coming back and was 2 down again. Johnny messed up the eighth, we halved the ninth, and I finally squared at the short twelfth.

Then I made a couple of fatal mistakes, just when I seemed to be getting the match in hand.

Johnny's iron second was bunkered at the thirteenth and I proceeded to pump one into the sand also, eventually having to hop a stymie to get a half in 5. Johnny pulled his second into some trees at the long fourteenth and I was nearly as close in 2 as he was in 3. I tried to pitch close over a bunker, cut the pitch six inches too fine, and was trapped, so my valiant effort to pick up a birdie 4 resulted in a buzzard 6, while Johnny holed a six-footer for a par 5 to go 1 up again. I thought I had a chance to catch him at the fifteenth, when his iron second was bunkered back of the green, but he came out well, holed another six-footer for the half in 4, and after that he played impeccable golf. His spoon drive at the dangerous seventeenth was as fine a shot as I ever saw, hole-high and ten feet from the stick on a mere ribbon of green. I was just outside him and my putt for a 2 rimmed the cup but stayed up. He nearly holed his to end the match, and closed

Bobby usually got an old fashioned home coming reception on return to his native Atlanta, Ga.

A boyish Bobby Jones looked every inch the winner.

me out with a perfectly played par 5 at the last hole, which I achieved loosely in the same figure.

Harrison Johnston, playing steady golf and winning two extra-hole matches, defeated Dr. Willing in the finals.

I cannot praise the California courses too extravagantly. The turf on the fairways is especially delightful, holding up the ball so consistently that I do not remember finding a really tight lie in the Golden State. The California putting surfaces, mostly of Cocoos bent, afford a wonderful texture, yet it was a curious fact that all the players from east of the Rockies experienced difficulty in getting the line consistently.

Bob Zuppke, football coach at Illinois, landscape painter, and quite a golfer, had a bizarre and yet possible explanation for this.

"It's not the greens," he told me. "It's the California skyline. Did you notice it specially? All zigzag—naked mountain ranges, the lines intersecting at all sorts of angles.

"Whether you notice it or not, the constant vision of zigzags on the horizon affects your perspective. You see tiny slopes that aren't there, or maybe you see a slant one way and it's the other. Did you miss a lot of ten-footers you thought you ought to have holed?"

Come to think of it, I did. Still, that had happened east of the Rockies.

So I went out to Del Monte with a chance at three records. I might have won my fifth amateur championship. I might have made it three national amateurs in a row. And I might have equaled Chick Evans' record of winning the open and the amateur the same season.

Instead of these, I made another record. I got licked in the first round.

However, I had something to remember from Winged Foot. In 1929 I had been national champion seven years in succession. There was a good deal of comfort in that.

53

Jack Dempsey's Hardest Fight

by Robert Edgren

Jack Dempsey, who at one time was Sports editor of Liberty Magazine, relates his actual thoughts in what he called his hardest fight.

"Yes," said Jack Dempsey, "you can say the Firpo fight was my hardest. But use your own judgment. They're all hard when the other fellow manages to pop you on the button. The only easy fight is where you walk out and let one punch go and the bird in front of you hits the floor and stretches out for a ten count the way Carl Morris did at New Orleans.

"What you want is my mental picture of my hardest fight. Is that it? Well, I'll tell you; it isn't much of a picture. The beginning is clear and the end is clear, but the middle is just a fog. Before the fight, in the afternoon, I was down along Riverside Drive, in New York City, playing on the grass with a lot of kids. I wasn't any more nervous about the fight than I would have been over shooting a squirrel with a buffalo gun.

"My plans were all made. I intended to watch Firpo's right hand like a hawk—watch his left hand, too. I was going to move fast, feint, and make him miss. Then when he'd missed me a few times and was floundering and leaving a good, clean opening you could toss a flower pot through—sock!—right on the button! Doc Kearns had it figured I couldn't miss getting him in the first round if I didn't slip on a banana peel and break my leg, and you know how Doc picks 'em.

"I got up there in the ring, and the crowd didn't bother me half as much as two waiters at my table during lunch. I'm getting used to crowds. I was sitting there looking over at Firpo and wondering whether he'd rush me at the start or wait for me to come to him when I began to notice something. I didn't get it at first. There was a lot of yelling and cheering and crowd noises and telegraph instruments going, and all that sort of thing, same as usual.

"Then, all of a sudden, it struck me. I wasn't being razzed. Nobody at all razzed me. Nobody in all that crowd! They weren't yelling at me; they were yelling for me. For the first time since Toledo I had all the crowd with me. Not like Jersey City, where a lot of people wanted the Frenchman to knock me dead, or Shelby, where I half expected some nut to take a shot at me.

"Then Joe Humphreys gave me that fine introduction, and the crowd yelled so all I could hear was the air shaking, like being under Niagara Falls. Then I got it. I wasn't only Jack Dempsey fighting for a lot of money. I was an American defending a title and I had to make good.

"Funny, that cheer nearly got me licked. If I'd been razzed, being used to that, I'd have gone out thinking of nothing but Jack Dempsey's own private interests and how to make Firpo miss a couple of times and leave the opening I wanted. Now I forgot my plans and decided to make good for that cheer by knocking Firpo out with the first punch. The first punch! Get that!

"I leaned over and looked for Firpo's softest spot and figured how to sock him there with the first sock.

Hit 'Em In The Solar Plexus

"The bell rang. Firpo got up and started toward me, slowly. I was, maybe, two steps from Luis when I saw his arm raised too high and his body left wide open——a mark like a barn door. I could see the edge of his ribs bordering the old solar plexus Fitz discovered—the surest knock-out spot there is. Hit 'em on the jaw and they may get up and crown you, but hit 'em in the pit of the stomach, right, and they stay where they drop.

"I jumped in to get Firpo before he could lower his guard.

"I threw everything from my shoestrings up into a left hook.

"I missed.

"Something smacked me, from somewhere. I felt my knees hit the floor and kind of bounce. No, I didn't slip that first time. I was knocked down. That's where I told you my head was knocked out and my legs weren't. I saw in the pictures afterward that I bounced up against him and went on fighting. But if you want to

Jack Dempsey climbs back into the ring after being knocked out of it by Firpo.

tell about that you'll have to do it yourself. What I remember is nothing—just nothing at all—a blank.

"Next I knew I was looking through a thick fog and Firpo was on the floor. I can't remember how many times he went down—seven, they say—but I know it was more than once, because I saw him on his stomach, and rolling on his back, and on his hands and knees—all different pictures—through the fog.

"I heard the referee telling me to go to my corner, and the ring was spinning around so fast I'd dive for the first corner I saw and grab the ropes to steady myself, and look for Doc Kearns. Only once I saw a flat, white face, kind of hazy, through the ropes, and I knew that was Doc, but I couldn't get any message over. And then I was fighting again.

"I don't remember when Firpo knocked me down the second time. I remember I felt the ropes against my back, and I was ducking punches, and I knew Firpo was throwing them at me, but the fog was so thick I couldn't see him. The fog, of course, was just local, you might say. I got that way from being socked. But I guess Luis Angel wasn't much better off.

"I didn't feel the punch that knocked me out of the ring. It must have been half a push, for if I'd been hit right with a snappy blow I'd never have been able to climb back. I felt the back of my head hit something. Luckily, it wasn't a typewriter.

"Then the fog turned black and a big yellow glow came through it, like the sun rising over a mountain ridge and shining down into a deep canyon. Then two black lines came across the sun, and all of a sudden I knew they were the ropes and the sun was the overhead picture

lights, and the big black blur that moved between me and the sun was Firpo looking down on me, and I'd been knocked out of the ring and had to hustle fast to get back in there in time to win.

Back Into the Ring

"So I grabbed something and scrambled up and slid through the ropes and away while Firpo was punching at me. My head was clearing and the fog half lifted, but I couldn't see him very plainly. I saw his punches coming, slow, slow, and thought I was swaying, fast and clever, getting away from them, but he kept pushing me back and I couldn't stop and stand against him. That made me mad. I felt the strength coming back into my arms and hooked him a good one that jarred my shoulder.

"I dropped something there, because the next thing I remember I had an awful whiff of the smelling salts that nearly took the top off my head, and half jumped out of my chair and found I was sitting in my corner. Doc Kearns was talking to me.

" 'You're slipping, Jack; you're slipping. Go get him,' Doc said.

"So I knew something serious must have happened, to worry Doc. Then my head was clear and it was just like starting the fight again. That ends the story."

"Well, go on," I said to Dempsey. "Give us your picture of the second round. There was another round, you know."

"O, that," said Dempsey indifferently. "I just went back to my original plan; made him miss, and knocked him out. I ought to have done it the first time."

POLITICS AND POLITICIANS

President Woodrow Wilson detested war with every fibre of his being. On March, 1913, the day of his inauguration, he put his right hand on the Bible determined that his country would never need to fire a shot in offense or even defense. Yet slowly, inexorably, and sadly, he became entangled in the vicious web of World War I. In April 1917, he declared war before Congress, then went back to the White House and wept. War kills some men and injures others. Wilson was one of the injured—a walking wounded who found it impossible to delegate tasks and tried to do too much himself. Yet one dream sustained him: after the war a League of Nations would guarantee peace forever. Sustained by this hope he went to Paris to aid in drawing up the peace treaty with Germany. It was another task he should have delegated, for the strain of the peace conference wore him out.

Yet the idea of the League of Nations still drove him on. Returning to this country, he found powerful forces arrayed against the League. The shock was too much and—as we see here—the President broke physically, launching the country into two years of dark drama when his wife was the strong, functioning person in the White House.

Yes—to all intents and purposes, a woman was once President of the United States!

Wilson viewed his mission as clean-cut, inspired by God. Russians like Lenin, Trotsky, and Stalin took an opposite view, for in that far-off country Byzantine intrigue was old as history. With the Czars overthrown in 1917, Lenin and Trotsky began the struggle for control of a rudderless land. The world watched in fascination, and suddenly a third figure appeared. His name was Josef Stalin and he turned out to be a master of iron ruthlessness, the man who came out on top.

But how did he do it? No one knew better than Leon Trotsky, who may have lost out to Lenin and Stalin, but always retained his sharp intellect and strong analytical powers.

We are about to enter upon a new period of liberalism and of sane reform in the United States, and we shall require unity of purpose, if not of opinion, if we are to achieve permanent and practical results. The United States has become a great nation, and its economic life functions along national lines, where our political life still clings too much to the political machinery of the past. As President of the United States I shall do my utmost, in coöperation with the people and with their chosen representatives, to restore the balance of our economic interests and to simplify and vitalize our political institutions, so that as changes come they may be effected without injury to the proper rights of any individual and without conflict with the spirit of American institutions. With your help, I can do it.

—*Franklin D. Roosevelt*

When A Woman Was President

by George Sylvester Viereck

George Sylvester Viereck wrote widely on domestic and foreign affairs. This article, written in 1928, was the first public revelation of what went on inside the White House in 1919-20 when President Wilson lay ill.

For six and one-half months, from September 26, 1919, to April 13, 1920, a woman was virtually President of the United States.

For six and one-half months Edith Bolling Wilson fulfilled the dream of Susan B. Anthony. She was, so to speak, not only acting President, but secretary to the President, and Secretary of State.

Between September 26 and October 4, when Wilson was paralyzed by a blood clot on the brain, Mrs. Wilson assumed the reins, and she remained in command from that day until April 13, 1920, when Wilson resumed meetings with his Cabinet. But she remained his coregent until the end, March 4, 1921.

If Mrs. Wilson did not virtually rule the United States throughout that period, who did?

From the very beginning misleading accounts of the President's condition appeared in the press. The deception began with Wilson's collapse on the train. Grayson called the President's trouble "nervous exhaustion" and added that it was "not alarming." Tumulty declared that the President's exertions had brought on a "nervous reaction in his digestive organs."

The following day Edith Bolling Wilson and Admiral Grayson were in control on the President's train.

No one, not even Senator Hitchcock, Wilson's personal spokesman in the Senate, saw Wilson after his arrival in Washington, September 29. On October 3 the visit of the specialists summoned to the President's bedside was noted in the press. The President's son-in-law, William G. McAdoo, arrived in Washington. He left, according to the dispatches, without being permitted to see his father-in-law.

Official statements were lacking in candor. While Wilson lay unconscious and paralyzed, the newspapers indicated that the President was "chafing under restraint." Grayson was "constantly with him." On October 6 the public heard that Mrs. Wilson and Grayson still "guarded" the President, who was so anxious to get to work that he had called for a stenographer, but had been persuaded to give up the idea.

In the absence of authentic news from the White House, rumors sprang up overnight like mushrooms. Press and public foundered in a sea of uncertainty.

A Bombshell Explodes

On October 10, 1919, Washington dispatches once more pictured a President improved to the point of being apparently about to overrule his physicians and wife and get back to work. But this picture was greatly changed by the Washington dispatches of October 12. The Associated Press story, carried by both the New York Times and the New York Tribune, began:

"Hope that President Wilson might soon regain his normal health and resume fully the duties of his office was swept away today by his physicians."

"The President," read a bulletin signed by Grayson, Ruffin, Stitt, and Dercum, "shows signs of continued improvement, but his condition is such as to necessitate his remaining in bed for an extended period."

On this same date a bombshell exploded— the first guarded challenge to those who, keeping the physical person of the President virtually prisoner, insisted on retaining control of the executive business of the country in his hands, or ostensibly in his hands. The charge of T.N.T. was the publication of a letter written by Senator George Higgins Moses of New Hampshire to a friend in Manchester in his home state.

The sensational nature of Senator Moses' allegations lost nothing in the elaboration in the Providence Journal of October 13:

President Wilson is suffering from a very dangerous cerebral hemorrhage. . . . There is partial physical paralysis and the brain lesion is of such a character that Mr. Wilson has suffered several periods of aphasia. . . . From a high government official . . . it is learned that even if the President should show signs of improvement by the gradual absorption of the hemorrhage, any mental strain . . . would mean . . . a more dangerous condition. It is also declared there is no possibility that Mr. Wilson would be able to perform the functions of his office either in the immediate or the remote future.

D. F. Houston confirms Mr. Palmer's statement. We learn from his book Eight Years With Wilson's Cabinet that the Vice President of the United States, like the Cabinet, was ignored by the guardians of the bedchamber.

The then President and Mrs. Wilson out for a Sunday afternoon stroll.

Responsible government officials began to feel that the President's case should be considered as one of "disability," requiring Congressional action. The American people, noted by Northcliffe to be docile, began to grumble. Faced with this situation, the physicians gave out longer, apparently franker, but really no more revealing bulletins. The New York Herald of October 16 printed an "unofficial explanation" to the effect that "the President is being kept in very general touch with affairs, but he is not permitted to know any details of the treaty fight. . . . Dr. Grayson and Mrs. Wilson inform the President in a general way what is happening."

Wilson Kept in Ignorance

An Associated Press dispatch from Washington lets the cat out of the bag. "With the exception of the news furnished him by Mrs. Wilson, the President has learned very little of national and international developments."

A writer in the Tribune uses stronger language on Sunday, October 19: "The ingenuity of his [the President's] retinue was taxed with appearing to carry out his wishes, while secretly thwarting them."

On October 21 the President for the first time performed an executive function (according to a headline in the Tribune) by appointing Owen D. Young of Schenectady to a vacant place in the Industrial Conference then going on in Washington. The Times account of the same incident has this significant passage: "It was learned at the White House that during the day the President had occasion to send for some papers of an official character which he went over with Mrs. Wilson. Mrs. Wilson does most of the President's reading for him, as the physicians do not wish to have him do his own reading at this time."

On this day also the newspapers carried the story that four bills had become laws without the President's signature and in default of any action by him, because these bills had not been laid before him and he had not been permitted to know about them. "It is explained that . . . these bills . . . were not presented to him under the policy of keeping as much business as possible from him." (New York Times, October 21.) Evidently it lay in Mrs. Wilson's hands to submit or to

Mrs. Edith Bolling Wilson—was she President of the U.S.?

withhold from the President legislation passed by the Congress.

On November 18 a curious dramatic situation occurred. The President was permitted, for the second time since he had been stricken, to sun himself on the south lawn of the White House. "From the windows of the Cabinet room the members of the Cabinet, while in session, could see the President in his wheel chair." They could see him but not reach or communicate with him. Senator Gilbert M. Hitchcock was equally unlucky. He led the fight for the Treaty that was most dear to Wilson's heart, but the sick room was locked against him.

On November 30 the Times reported that the President's physicians, after consultation, would not allow him to hold a conference scheduled with Senator Hitchcock at that time.

On December 3—more than two months after the breakdown in Wichita—the Times recorded that Hitchcock was still barred from the President. Those close to President Wilson were quoted as stating that the condition of his health was improving steadily. But "a considerable number of congressmen believe that the President is in much worse condition than his physicians have indicated."

Upheld by the warm, firm hand of a woman —the woman who was President—the palsied hand of Woodrow Wilson clung desperately to power. Edith Bolling Wilson had no political ambitions. But events conspired with her vanity to perpetuate her reign. Woodrow Wilson's intellectual self lay dormant; his practical self was asleep; his emotional self, wide awake, was the vassal of his moral self. His emotions and his conscience convinced him that he could, even from his sick bed, entice America to accept his cherished Covenant.

Edith Bolling Wilson nurtured this illusion.

"Never," Colonel House remarked to me, "was there a more devoted wife." Mrs. Wilson's predominant desire was to shield Wilson from pain. But surely, below the threshold of consciousness other motives came into play. The purple which Mrs. Wilson had affected in Paris became the color of a queen regnant. While Wilson was on his back she exercised the functions of the President alone. When he was able to participate, she shared with him the government of the United States. No senator, no member of the Cabinet, not the President's own secretary, could gain a glimpse of Wilson without her permission. Her whim decided whether a king or an ambassador was to be received, whether a bill awaiting the President's signature would become law or not.

Wilson Wanted Other Friends

Wilson, judging by echoes from his sick-bed conversations, sometimes longed for other friends; but he did not have the strength or the courage to summon them. No act of Woodrow Wilson from this period until the end of his life was undertaken without the knowledge and consent of Edith Bolling Wilson.

With shaky hand Wilson signed the few letters and documents placed before him by his wife. Everything likely to disturb his peace of mind was withheld. Nevertheless, there were days when he cried and wept like a child. His oldest daughter, Margaret, assisted his wife. Their devotion kept the flickering flame burning. Mrs. Wilson, remarks the astute David Lawrence, stood between her husband and the government, indeed between him and the outside world. "Even the private secretary, Mr.

Tumulty, refrained from entering the bedchamber except when sent for. He placed his memoranda on vital questions before Mrs. Wilson, leaving it to her to discover the proper moment to ask the President for his opinion or decision. *She was, so to speak, the reigning monarch."*

Even before he came under the sway of Edith Bolling Galt, Woodrow Wilson was strongly susceptible to wifely influence. He was, William Allen White remarks in his penetrating study, tremendously uxorious. Marriage, like friendship, was a crutch upon which he leaned heavily. Without his first wife, Ellen Axson, he would have remained a teacher in a girls' school. Princeton, Trenton, Washington would have remained daydreams. Ellen Axson, McAdoo says, was the only human being who fully understood Wilson. Wilson himself spoke of her as the most radiant creature he had ever known.

In spite of her strong artistic personality, Ellen Axon possessed the supreme gift of self-effacement. Without this she would have resented the predominating influence of Colonel House. She not only encouraged that friendship but countenanced her husband's "flirtations" with Mrs. Hulbert (Peck). Wilson needed feminine sympathy. When Ellen Axson died he wrote at once to Mary Hulbert that he wanted her to be the first to know. When he was betrothed to Mrs. Galt, Mrs. Hulbert was his first confidante. After his second marriage the correspondence with Mary Hulbert lapsed and his friendship with House lost its glow.

Wifely Devotion Heroic

Feminine devotion usually includes a strong sense of possessiveness. This sense of possessiveness was evidently more marked in the second than in the first Mrs. Wilson. Tumulty, who has no reason to love Edith Bolling Wilson, pays a touching tribute to the heroic quality of her devotion:

As woman and wife, the first thought of her mind and the first care of her heart must be for his health. Once, at an acute period of his illness, certain officials insisted that they must see him because they carried information which it was "absolutely necessary that the President of the United States should have,"

and she quietly replied: "I am not interested in the President of the United States. I am interested in my husband and his health!"

But, in spite of her devotion to her husband, Edith Bolling Wilson did not relish the thought of permitting Wilson to exchange the White House for a sanatorium. She had tasted the sweet draft of power. She had basked in the sunshine of high station. If she had been asked to sacrifice both to save Wilson's life, she would not have hesitated an instant. But the human mind is so constituted that problems do not present themselves in this undisguised fashion. Her own ambition assumed the shape of his. She persuaded herself that for his sake, not hers, she must keep up the pretext that Wilson was still actively President of the United States.

In December, 1919, two or three months after the breakdown, Franklin K. Lane, Secretary of the Interior, wrote to a friend: "The President is getting better slowly, but we communicate with him almost entirely through his doctor [Grayson]." In another letter, the same month, Lane enlarges upon the same topic. "Things," he assures his correspondent, "are going well notwithstanding the President's illness. No one is satisfied that we know the truth, and every dinner table is filled with speculation. Some say paralysis, and some say insanity. Grayson tells me it is nervous breakdown, whatever that means. He is, however, getting better, and meantime the Cabinet is running things."

Lane wished to resign in order to accept an offer of a lucrative position. For months he was kept from this action by the inaccessibility of the President. At last, on January 5, he put his dilemma before Rear Admiral Grayson. He asked him to "be perfectly frank" in advising him what to do, as he did not wish to "do anything to hurt our Chief." Three months or more after the thrombosis that laid Wilson low, a Cabinet officer cannot approach his superior except through this young doctor-admiral! It is difficult to reconcile this situation with the statement that Wilson carried on the duties imposed upon him by the Chief Magistracy of the Republic. There are witnesses galore to the contrary.

No member of the Cabinet was more devoted to Wilson than Houston. Wilson himself, in a letter to House, wishes that there were more

An ailing President Wilson poses with his cabinet.

than one Houston. Both Wilson and Mrs. Wilson reposed their trust in the Secretary of Agriculture. Yet Houston did not have access to Wilson. And it was Mrs. Wilson who offered him the Treasury. Houston himself tells how, one morning (January 25, 1920) when he awoke with the grippe, he received a summons to the White House from her, bidding him call at four-thirty in the afternoon.

He telephoned Mrs. Wilson and expressed the fear that he might carry with him the danger of infection. She insisted, however, upon his visit.

When he arrived, the mistress of the White House received him graciously in the sitting room. The conversation skipped from one topic to another until the servants had cleared away the tea table. Then she said:

"You are wondering why I wanted to see you and why I sent for you this afternoon. Of course you know that I did not ask you to take the trouble to come merely to drink tea. The President asked me to tell you that he is very anxious for you to accept the Secretaryship of the Treasury. He is reluctant to have you give up Agriculture, but still thinks he now needs you more in the Treasury . . ."

Houston said: "Please give my greetings to the President and tell him that I am very grateful to him for this further evidence of his confidence. I am in the harness until March 4, 1921, if he wishes it, and as long as I am with him I will dig stumps, or act as Secretary of the Treasury, or assume any other task he assigns me."

"That is very interesting. That is just what the President said you would say."

Houston continues:

Mrs. Wilson said that the President would like to know whether I had anybody in mind to suggest for Secretary of Agriculture. I asked if he was thinking about anybody. She answered: "Yes; Meredith."

Houston discussed this tentative selection, and suggested President W.O. Thompson of the University of Ohio as another possibility. His account goes on:

She then asked whether I had anybody in

mind whom I could suggest for the position of Secretary of the Interior. She added: "The President is somewhat embarrassed. Secretary Lane has resigned—in the press. The President has not yet been offically informed of his going. He would like your judgment."

It is difficult to escape the conclusion that in this period, the fifth month of Wilson's disability, Mrs. Wilson was his regent. Grayson, too, enters into the picture the following month. Houston reports how, on February 14, he discussed with Dr. Grayson the desirability of the President's filling vacancies on the Tariff Commission, and sent certain messages to Wilson through Dr. Grayson.

When Grayson told him that the President had asked for Lansing's resignation, Houston was not surprised.

"Do you know," he asked, "who will succeed the Secretary of State?"

Grayson did not know.

"The President is very much worried. In fact, he is worrying himself sick over the matter."

"Why?"

"Because the President is no longer in a position to write his notes and papers as he formerly was, and he wants somebody who has great facility in this direction."

Houston suggested Frank Polk. However, the following morning the appointment of Bainbridge Colby was announced in the papers. To what extent was Wilson consulted? Was his mind able to grasp the facts presented to him by Mrs. Wilson?

The convalescing president and his wife are driven about the capital.

The stricken Wilson had only a few years to live after leaving the White House.

Although Mrs. Wilson acted only in the name of the President, some communications from the White House bore her signature. "Please bear in mind," says Frank L. Polk, the legal adviser of the State Department, "that I was in Paris as head of the American Peace Delegation from the middle of July, 1919, to the middle of December, so I have no personal knowledge as to what took place immediately after Mr. Wilson was taken ill. On my return from Paris, communications from the White House were signed by the President and *in some instances by Mrs. Wilson. But* the letters I wrote the President in regard to foreign affairs would have notes in pencil on the margin in his handwriting, approving or disapproving the suggestions therein contained. I understand he communicated with the Cabinet through Mrs. Wilson, Mr. Tumulty, and by notes signed by himself."

Wilson may have scribbled consent or disagreement on the margins of the notes submitted by the State Department. But after his stroke, as White remarks, the world practically was shut off from Woodrow Wilson. "And when the public was shut away from him, he knew nothing of the truth about public sentiment in the country. It was as though the curtain had fallen upon him with the roar of applause which greeted his speech at Pueblo always reverberating in his heart."

Wilson's will left his fortune entirely to his wife, except for an annuity of $2,500 to Margaret, his eldest daughter. Under the terms of the will marriage would deprive Margaret Wilson even of this little stipend. His will seemed all the more incredible to his friends since Edith Bolling Wilson was reputed to possess a fortune in her own right, and since there was no question of the mutual devotion which existed between Woodrow Wilson and his three daughters. Wilson, kept by wartime from entertaining, had saved a large part of his salary. He was very well-to-do when he died. The total value of his estate was estimated to be more than $600,000.

Did Stalin Poison Lenin?

by Leon Trotsky

Leon Trotsky was in exile in Mexico when this piece appeared in the August 1940 Liberty magazine. He was revealing his behind-the-scenes knowledge of Russia and the revolution in books and magazine articles until he was brutally murdered.

During the ten years of my present exile the Kremlin's literary agents have systematically relieved themselves of the need to answer anything I write about the U.S.S.R. by alluding to my "hatred" of Stalin. Yet Stalin and I have been separated by events so fiery that they have consumed in flames and reduced to ashes everything personal. Stalin is my enemy. But Hitler, too, is my enemy, and so is Mussolini, and so are many others. Today there remains in me as little personal feeling toward Stalin as toward General Franco or the Mikado.

I present in this article startling facts from the story of how a provincial revolutionist became the dictator of a great country. Every fact I mention, every reference and quotation, can be substantiated either by official Soviet publications or by documents preserved in my archives.

The last period of Lenin's life was filled with intense conflict between him and Stalin, which culminated in a complete break between them. As always, there was nothing in any way personal about Lenin's hostility toward Stalin. But as time went on, Stalin took increasing advantage of the opportunities his post presented for revenging himself upon his opponents. Little by little, Lenin became convinced that certain of Stalin's traits were directly inimical to the party. From that matured his decision to reduce Stalin to a rank-and-file member of the Central Committee.

Lenin's health took a sudden turn for the worse toward the end of 1921. The first stroke came in May, 1922. For two months he was unable either to move, to speak, or to write. In July he began to convalesce slowly. In October he returned from the country to the Kremlin and took up his work again. In December he opened fire against Stalin's persecu-tions. He came out against Stalin on the question of foreign trade monopoly and was preparing for the forthcoming party congress an address which would be "a bombshell against Stalin."

"Let us speak frankly," wrote Lenin on March 2. "The Commissariat of Inspection does not today enjoy the slightest authority. . . . There is no worse institution among us than our People's Commissariat of Inspection." At the head of the Inspection was Stalin. He well understood the implications of such language.

In the middle of December, 1922, Lenin's health obliged him to absent himself from the conference. Stalin at once hid from Lenin much information. Measures of blockade were insti-tuted against persons closest to Lenin. Lenin was aflame with alarm and indignation. His chief source of worry was Stalin, whose be-havior became bolder as the reports of physi-cians about Lenin's health became less favor-able. In those days Stalin was morose, snarling, his pipe firmly clenched between his teeth, a sinister gleam in his jaundiced eyes. His fate was at stake.

Several lines dictated by Lenin on March 5, 1923, to a trusted stenographer announced dryly the severance of "all personal and com-radely relations with Stalin." That note is the last surviving Lenin document. The very next night he again lost his power of speech.

The so-called Lenin "testament" was written in two installments during his second illness: on December 25, 1922, and on January 4, 1923. "Stalin, having become Secretary Gen-eral," declares the testament, "has concen-trated an enormous power in his hands, and I am not sure that he always knows how to use that power with sufficient caution." Ten days later Lenin added: "I propose to the comrades to find a way to remove Stalin from that position and appoint to it another man" who would be "more loyal, less capricious," etc.

Lenin Asked for Poison?

When Stalin first read the text be broke into a rage against Lenin. The testament not only failed to terminate the internal struggle, which was what Lenin wanted, but increased it to a feverish pitch. Stalin could no longer doubt that Lenin's return to activity would mean his own political death. Only Lenin's death could clear the way for him.

I followed the course of Lenin's second illness day by day through the physician we had in common, Dr. Gaitier.

"Is it possible, Fedor Alexandrovich, that this is the end?" my wife and I would ask him time and again.

"That cannot be said at all. Vladimir Ilyich can get on his feet again. He has a powerful organism."

"And his mental faculties?"

"Basically, they will remain untouched. Not every note, perhaps, will keep its former purity, but the virtuoso will remain a virtuoso."

Yet at a meeting of the Politburo members, Zinoviev, Kamenev, and myself, Stalin informed us, after the departure of the secretary, that Lenin had suddenly called him in and had asked him for poison. Lenin was again losing the faculty of speech, considered his situation hopeless, foresaw the approach of a new stroke, did not trust his physicians. His mind was perfectly clear and he suffered unendurably.

I recall how extraordinary, enigmatic, and out of tune with the circumstances Stalin's face seemed to me then. A sickly smile was fixed on it, as a mask. I see before me the pale and silent Kamenev, who sincerely loved Lenin, and Zinoviev, bewildered, as at all difficult moments. Had they known about Lenin's request? Or had Stalin sprung this as a surprise on his allies in the triumvirate as well as on me?

"Naturally, we cannot even consider carrying out this request!" I exclaimed. "Gaitier has not lost hope. Lenin can still recover."

"I told him all that," Stalin replied, not without a touch of annoyance. "But he wouldn't listen to reason. The old man is suffering. He

Leon Trotsky was one of the masterminds of the Russian revolution.

says he wants to have the poison at hand. He'll use it when he is convinced that his condition is hopeless."

"The old man is suffering," Stalin repeated, staring vaguely past us. No vote was taken, since this was not a formal conference, but we parted with the implicit understanding that we could not even consider sending poison to Lenin.

"Anyway, it's out of the question," I insisted. "He might succumb to a passing mood and take the irrevocable step."

Only a few days before, Lenin had written his pitiless postscript to the testament. Several days later he broke off all personal relations with Stalin. Why should he turn to Stalin, of all people, with his tragic request? The answer is simple: He saw in Stalin the only man who would grant it, since Stalin was directly interested in doing so. At the same time, it is possible that he wanted to test Stalin: just how eagerly would Stalin take advantage of this opportunity? In those days Lenin thought not only of death but of the fate of the party.

69

But did Lenin actually ask Stalin for poison? Was the whole version not invented by Stalin to prepare his alibi? He could have had no reason to fear a verification, for no one could question the sick Lenin.

More than ten years before the notorious Moscow trials Stalin had confessed to Kamenev and Dzerzhinsky, his allies of that time, that his highest delight in life was to keep a keen eye on an enemy, prepare everything painstakingly, mercilessly revenge himself, and then go to sleep.

During the last big trial, staged in March, 1938, a special place in the prisoners' dock was occupied by Henry Yagoda. Some secret bound Stalin to Yagoda, who had worked in the Cheka and the GPU for sixteen years, at first as an assistant chief, later as the head, and all the time as Stalin's most trusted aide against the opposition. The system of confes-sions to crimes that had never been committed is Yagoda's handiwork, if not his brainchild. In 1933 Stalin rewarded Yagoda with the Order of Lenin, in 1935 elevated him to the rank of Commissar General of State Defense—that is, Marshal of the Political Police. In Yagoda's person was elevated a nonentity, held in contempt by all. The old revolutionists exchanged looks of indignation.

At the time of the great "purge" Stalin decided to liquidate his fellow culprit who knew too much. In April, 1937, Yagoda was arrested and eventually executed.

It was revealed at that trial that Yagoda, a former pharmacist, had a special poison cabinet from which he would bring out vials and entrust them to his agents. He had at his disposal several toxicologists, for whom he organized a special laboratory, providing it with means without limit and without control. It is,

V. I. Lenin, one of the founders of the Soviet Union at a Bolshevik rally.

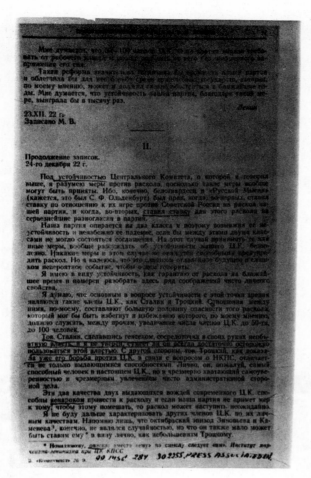

A photograph of Lenin's will.

of course, unthinkable that Yagoda might have established such an enterprise for his own personal needs.

Suspicions that Stalin had somewhat aided the destructive force of nature in the case of Maxim Gorky sprang up directly after the great writer's death. A concomitant task of Yagod's trial was to clear Stalin of that suspicion. Hence the repeated declarations by Yagoda, the physicians, and the other accused, that Gorky was "a close friend of Stalin," "a trusted person," an enthusiastic "Stalinist." If only half of this were true, Yagoda would not have taken it upon himself to kill Gorky, and still less would he have entrusted such a plot to a Kremlin physician, who could have destroyed him by simply telephoning Stalin.

During the days of the trial, the accusations, like the confessions, seemed phantasmagoric to me. Subsequent information and analysis forced me to alter that judgment. Not every-

thing in the trials was a lie. Not all the poisoners were sitting in the prisoners' dock. The chief among them was conducting the trial by telephone. It is only Yagoda who has disappeared; his poison cabinet remains.

At the 1938 trial Stalin charged Bukharin with having prepared in 1918 an attempt on Lenin's life. The naïve and ardent Bukharin venerated Lenin, worshiped him, could not have had personal ambitious designs. All the accusations of the Moscow trials are cut to this pattern. Stalin sees the best means to dispel suspicions against himself in ascribing the crime to his adversary and forcing him to "confess."

Lenin asked for poison—if he really did—at the end of February, 1923. In the beginning of March he was again paralyzed. But his powerful organism, supported by his inflexible will, reasserted itself. Toward winter he began to improve slowly, to move about more freely; he listened to reading and read himself; his faculty of speech began to come back to him. The findings of the physicians became increasingly more hopeful.

Stalin was after power, all of it, come what might. He already had a firm grip on it. His goal was near, but the danger emanating from Lenin was even nearer. At his side was the pharmacist Yagoda.

The news of Lenin's death found me and my wife en route to the Caucasus, where I hoped to get rid of an infection, the nature of which still remains a mystery to my physicians. I immediately telegraphed to the Kremlin: "I deem it necessary to return to Moscow. When is the funeral?" The reply came in about an hour: "The funeral will take place on Saturday. You will not be able to return on time. The Politburo thinks that because of the state of your health you must proceed to Sukhum. Stalin." Why this hurry? Why precisely Saturday? But I did not feel that I should request postponement of the funeral for my sake alone. Only in Sukhum did I learn that it had been changed to Sunday.

It was safer in all respects to keep me away until the body had been embalmed and the viscera cremated.

When I asked the physicians in Moscow about the immediate cause of Lenin's death,

72

which they had not expected, they were at a loss to account for it. The autopsy was carried out with all the necessary rites: Stalin took care of this himself. But the surgeons did not search for poison. They understood that politics stand above medicine.

I did not renew personal relations with Zinoviev and Kamenev until two years later, after they had broken with Stalin. They avoided all discussion of Lenin's death. Only Bukharin made now and then, *tête-à-tête*, unexpected and strange allusions. "Oh, you don't know Koba [Stalin]," he said with his frightened smile "Koba is capable of anything."

When the roof has collapsed and doors and windows have fallen off, a house is hard to live in. Today gusty drafts are blowing across our entire planet. All traditional principles of morality are increasingly worse off, and not only those emanating from Stalin. But a historical explanation is not a justification. Nero, too, was a product of his epoch. But after he perished his statues were smashed and his name was scraped off everything. The vengeance of history is more terrible than the vengeance of the most powerful Secretary General.

Lenin's body lies in state in Moscow while Trotsky was deceived into staying out of the city until after the funeral.

MEN, MONEY AND MACHINES

The economic revolution of the Twentieth Century could truly be captioned the era of MEN, MONEY AND MACHINES: the inventive minds of men such as Wilbur and Orville Wright, Thomas Edison and Albert Einstein; the money which gave impetus to the growth of corporate empires and conglomerates, which in turn shaped the economic destiny of America and delivered products to the world marketplace; and the machines that were to not only make our world "go 'round," but cause it to become a great deal smaller in the process.

More than any other event, the emergence of American technology and the expansion of our economic influence may surely be the most significant historical factors of the Twentieth Century.

Here you will find the stories of some remarkable men and the changes they have wrought with their minds, their money and their machines.

The Daring Young Men
by Major Lent

Major L. B. Lent collaborated with Orville Wright on this article which came out in 1928, a quarter century after man's first flight.

For as long as human progress shall have historians, a date, an event, and two names will be prominent in their chronicles.

The date is December 17, 1903. The event is the first controlled flight of a power-driven airplane. The two names are Orville and Wilbur Wright.

In 1910 the Wright brothers offered their Kitty Hawk airplane of 1903—the first power-driven plane that ever carried a pilot in free flight—to the Smithsonian Institution as a permanent exhibit. They were told that the officials would prefer a 1908 Wright airplane.

Meanwhile the institution had acquired and exhibited a model and the ill-fated 1903 "aërodrome," restored, of Samuel Pierpont Langley. Later on, the institution's label for the Langley machine offended Orville, and, in consequence of all this, he sent off the Wrights' first plane to a museum in England.

Last October the secretary of the Smithsonian published a conciliatory review of the controversy, with announcement that the label in question had been modified. Orville was not conciliated, however, as he showed in a statement to the Associated Press. He has always felt that his brother and he were treated unfairly by the Smithsonian authorities in the matter of credit for the discoveries that made flight possible.

Those who know him are convinced that his resentment is in behalf of Wilbur's memory more than in his own behalf.

Most people do not know just what the Wright brothers contributed to the solution of the problem of flight. Nor do they know what manner of man is this gentle soul who seems content to move along into his declining years, vividly recalled only by those who have immediately to do with his special branch of science. Few realize the tremendous struggle which gave us the airplane; even fewer know why these men succeeded when others, who had tried for years, had failed.

It has been my privilege and pleasure to spend much time with Orville Wright, to hear from his own lips the story of the achievement of himself and his brother, and to learn many other relevant things, yet I confess to an almost total inability to picture him in words and to convey his quiet charm.

The story should give a more satisfactory idea of the man than could any attempt at description.

The interest of the Wright brothers in aërial navigation dates from their childhood. In the late fall of 1878, their father came into the house one evening with some object concealed in his hands, and, before the boys could see what it was, tossed it in the air. Instead of falling, it flew to the end of the room until it struck the ceiling. It was the familiar mechanical toy known to science as the helicopter.

This fragile toy lasted but a short time in the hands of the boys, but its memory was abiding. As they grew older, they built their own helicopters, but discovered that the larger ones would not fly, little knowing then that a machine having only twice the linear dimensions of another required eight times the power.

Young Kite Expert

Next they turned their attention to kites and soon were recognized by all the boys in their part of Dayton as experts in building and flying them. In 1896, when these two young men were twenty-five and twenty-nine years old respectively, their eyes were caught by an item in the daily newspaper reporting the accidental death of Otto Lilienthal. He was killed by a fall from a glider of his own design and construction, after a long series of trials in an attempt to master the art of flying.

This rekindled their earlier boyish interest in the habits and powers of birds.

They reasoned that if such men as Leonardo da Vinci, the great universal genius; Sir George Cayley, Professor Langley, Dr. Alexander Graham Bell, and others had given serious consideration to this supposed impossibility, then man might some day really learn to fly.

Realizing that there were probably a large number of great difficulties to overcome, they felt that the cheapest and quickest way would be first to learn what others had experienced.

But the available literature disappointed them. Most of it was mere speculation, and later they were to find that it was very largely unsound and of little use to them.

The activity of other experimenters, quite intense during the period from 1889 to 1897, had produced no positive results and had largely subsided, the experimenters themselves practically retiring from the field acknowledging defeat. As for their published data, either it was entirely wrong, or else truth and error were so mixed as to make it impossible to separate them.

The first conclusion they arrived at was perhaps, in one sense, the most important. They correctly concluded that the lack of the abilities to control the balance of a flying machine and to guide its flight were the stumbling blocks in the path to success.

Both were quite satisfied, as were others at that time, that sufficient sustentation could be obtained to carry the necessary loads of an engine, fuel, operator, and other things.

Their second conclusion, which also was afterward proved sound, was that it was impracticable to maintain balance by shifting the weight of the operator to counteract the effect of gusts of wind or other forces. This had been attempted by Lilienthal and Pilcher in their trials with rigid gliders.

The Wrights saw that some way must be found to make the same forces of the wind which tended to overturn the plane bring it back to its proper flight position.

The world now knows that any other solution is practically impossible. They were the first to realize it.

Their belief in the correctness of this hypothesis was strengthened, if not confirmed, by trials on the kites with which they were constantly experimenting, and also by intelligent and careful observation of the flight of pigeons.

Search For an Airfield

As early as 1899 they fastened auxiliary strings to corners of box kites and so partially confirmed their theory of dynamic balance by warping the surfaces of these kites and controlling their movements.

They felt that if Lilienthal had, in five years of elapsed time, spent only about five minutes actually in the air, the important and essential thing was to *practice flying*; that after the art of flying gliders was acquired, it could be applied to power machines.

Accordingly it occurred to their resourceful minds to find some place where a constant prevailing wind of fifteen to twenty miles per hour would make it unnecessary to bring the machine back to the top of the hill for each glide, and so would enable them to practice by the hour.

As the Weather Bureau informed them that

the vicinity of Kitty Hawk, North Carolina, fulfilled the requirements, their first glider was taken there in the autumn of 1900. But the joke was on them, so to speak, for they soon found that while the *average* was about fifteen miles per hour, it was likely to be zero for three days and sixty on the fourth.

This first glider was quite different from any previously used by others. It embodied the ingenious arrangement of two superimposed wings (exactly as in our modern biplane) rigidly trussed along their front and rear edges, but not trussed from front to rear.

The lateral balance was to be controlled by warping the opposite sides of both sets of wings in opposite directions.

An auxiliary horizontal surface was mounted on a supporting frame in front of the lower wing. The rear edge of this auxiliary surface could be raised or lowered, producing the upward or downward curvature of the surface. This movement was to control the longitudinal, or fore and aft, balance. With machines of this description they made numerous experiments on the seashore near Kitty Hawk during 1900 and 1901.

Their experiences during these two seasons confirmed some of their ideas, but on the whole were very discouraging. In the words of Wilbur, "When we left Kitty Hawk at the end of 1901 we doubted that we would ever resume our experiments. At this time I made the prediction that men would sometime fly, but that it would not be within our lifetime."

But even then, for the first time in history, wings adjusted to different angles of incidence on the right and left sides had been successfully used in attempting to control the balance of a flying machine.

The brothers had accomplished more than any of their predecessors, but like them had found that the positive results obtained were too small for the effort and money expended. They were about ready to abandon the task and acknowledge defeat, as had the others.

Perhaps the most discouraging feature of the two seasons' trials was the discovery that data calculated by others was so unreliable that they might as well cast it all aside. The calculated "lifts" were nowhere realized in practice.

Discouraged as they were after returning home to Dayton in 1901, they could not keep

The interior of the Wright Brothers airplane factory at Dayton, Ohio.

their minds off the puzzling things which they had observed, nor could they keep from discussing possible solutions. Before long they were again as deeply interested as ever. They decided to work out complete data of their own. The winter of 1901-'02 was devoted to a series of laboratory investigations which were as ingenious, painstaking, and successful as any of which I have knowledge.

The First Wind Tunnel

Putting aside all precedent, they designed and constructed their own "wind tunnel" for testing miniature models, and a most effective balance for measuring relative reactions. With these instruments, they obtained data which they were able later to translate into results that could be applied in their designs.

They experimented with curved wing forms (most others had previously investigated the reactions of flat planes) and obtained data relating to the lift and drift of various wing forms.

They also, for the first time, made a systematic investigation of the effect of "aspect ratio" (the ratio of the total length, or span, of a wing to its breadth, or chord).

More than two hundred miniature wing surfaces were tried out. Not only were the characteristics of a great variety of wings investigated, but the relative resistances of struts of various shapes were determined. This last disclosed the great advantage of streamlining parts of the structure to decrease head resistance.

The labor expended in these experiments was more than repaid by the results obtained with the third glider which the brothers took to Kitty Hawk in August, 1902.

The nature of the journey to camp, involving a twenty-five hour trip by rail, a twenty-four hour trip on a sailing vessel, and lastly a small-boat trip, would have discouraged anyone less enthusiastic and persistent.

Almost a thousand glides were made between September 23 and October 28. Only one accident occurred. The following is from Orville Wright's diary entry of September 23, 1902:

The result was a heap of flying machine, cloth, and sticks, with me in the center, without a bruise or a scratch. The experiments thereupon suddenly came to a close till the repairs could be made. In spite of this sad catastrophe

we are tonight in a hilarious mood as a result of the encouraging performances of the machine, both in control and in angles of flight, which we are convinced will be at least three degrees better than any machine ever tried before.

Their laboratory work had been largely confirmed in practice. They now knew for certain that their methods of controlling balance were correct, that their data relating to lifts and resistances were sound, and that in a larger machine ample lift could be obtained to enable it to carry a power plant as well as the aviator. The very next step could take them to a power machine.

But a power plant for such a purpose did not exist.

While gas engines had enjoyed quite a period of development and were capable of generating considerable power per unit of weight, there were no such things as airplane propellers, nor was there any information about them.

These two related problems, of building a suitable gasoline engine, and constructing propellers or air screws, must be solved before the power machine could become a reality.

They first thought that their tables applying to wing design could be used in connection with the formulas for marine propellers, for air propellers were simply small wings traveling in a circular path. But they found that marine formulas were almost entirely empirical and the two conditions were not at all similar.

As Orville says, "With the machine moving forward, the air flying backward, the propellers turning sidewise, and nothing standing still, it seemed impossible to find a starting point from which to trace the various simultaneous reactions."

It was not until several months had passed, and every phase of the problems had been threshed out over and over, that the various reactions began to untangle themselves.

The first propellers, built entirely from the Wrights' calculations, gave efficiencies of better than 65 per cent—about one-third more than had been obtained by Maxim or Langley.

The first power machine was calculated to weigh 600 pounds, including the operator and an eight-horsepower engine. But the engine, on trial, developed nearly twelve horsepower and this permitted the addition of about 150 pounds

The Wright Brothers experiment with gliders at Kitty Hawk, North Carolina in 1902.

weight, making it possible to strengthen the wings and other parts.

The system of controls was the same as had been developed in the gliders. A power plant had been substituted for the force of gravity, to produce horizontal instead of inclined flight.

The first flights with this machine were made on December 17, 1903, on the beach near Kitty Hawk.

Only five persons besides the two brothers were present. While a general invitation to the few residents of that locality had been given, not many apparently cared to face the rigors of the cold December day in order to see another machine *not* fly.

Twenty Historic Seconds

The first flight lasted only twelve seconds, but it was *the first in the history of the world* in which a machine carrying a man had raised itself by its own power into the air in free flight; had sailed forward on a level course without reduction of speed; and had finally landed without being wrecked.

The second and third flights were a little longer. The fourth lasted fifty-nine seconds and covered a distance of 852 feet against a twenty-mile head wind—the first world's record for distance and duration.

The machine was carried back to camp and set down in what was thought to be a safe place, but a gust of wind caught it and it started to turn over. All hands made a rush, but arrived too late. The resulting damage was sufficient to stop further experiments for the time.

If the fates were ever generous to these two indomitable men, I have yet to discover it. But the end of their long struggle was in sight, the victory was already assured.

The spring of 1904 found them with a new and stronger machine continuing their experiments on what is known as Huffman Prairie at Simm's Station, eight miles east of Dayton. The first and second trials, to which newspapermen had been invited, were failures owing to engine trouble.

But from this time on progress was rapid. Longer and longer flights were made. For the first time in history, an airplane was flown around a closed path and back to its starting point. Soon they were making numerous circuits of the field, staying in the air longer, mastering the art of flying. The story of their achievements from this time on is too well known to need repetition.

Now, with the true story of this epic achievement in our minds, what are we to say of the men who did the job?

In order to emphasize the important features of this gigantic task, and to give a clearer perspective, I take the liberty of summarizing them:

The brothers' interest in flying was awakened in boyhood; it grew with the increased knowledge of what others had done or were doing; it passed from the curious stage to the active one; it became so intense as to force them on from one step to another until every obstacle had been forcibly thrust aside and the problem solved.

Instead of receiving any material aid from the experiences and researches of others, they were misled by what they tried to use and finally were forced to rely wholly upon their own efforts.

They grasped the salient and important points of this complex problem, where others had not.

They correctly diagnosed the difficulties and found the remedies.

Their progressive labors involved acquiring knowledge of the necessary mathematics and allied sciences, and the devising of laboratory apparatus and methods.

Their work was prompted entirely by their own interest in the subject and financed entirely from their own meager resources, earned principally in a bicycle shop they had.

If genius is, as Franklin said, an infinite capacity for taking pains, these two men are among the world's greatest.

Wilbur Wright flying at Pau, France.

Flying With Lindbergh

by Major Thomas G. Lanphier

Major Thomas G. Lanphier was one of the Lone Eagle's few close friends. He wrote this in 1938, after Lindy's life had been marred by the kidnapping of his infant son.

Aviation's foremost hero was Charles A. Lindbergh, affectionately known as Slim.

When Lindbergh made his famous flight in 1927, I was acting as commanding officer of the First Pursuit Group, stationed at Selfridge Field, Mount Clemens, Michigan. We received orders from the War Department to fly to Washington, D.C., to meet the battleship with was bringing this hero back, and to escort the illustrious pair "We"—Lindbergh and his plane, the Spirit of St. Louis—on the flight to New York.

Our squadron of twenty-four planes was in the air early for our mid-air rendezvous with Lindbergh. But the appointed hour came and went—and there was no sign of him. I led the squadron over the flying field where the Spirit of St. Louis had been disembarked. She was there all right, but mechanics were working on her. Her "prop" was dead. We pulled up and flew for another hour. By that time I had begun to worry about the amount of fuel in our tanks. So I gave the signal to land.

I had landed myself and was watching the rest of the squadron come in when suddenly I saw an army plane like our own taxiing out in front of a flight of three planes about to land.

One of the strictest rules of flying is that landing planes shall have the right of way. I rushed forward and grabbed the wing of the offending plane before it reached the runway. "Where do you think you're going? And who do you think you are?" I yelled angrily.

A Meek "I'm Lindbergh"

The man in the cockpit answered my second question first. "I'm Lindbergh," he said meekly.

Later that summer Lindbergh made his tour of the United States, under the auspices of the Guggenheim Foundation, for the purpose of stimulating interest in aviation. At various times during this tour the First Pursuit Group acted as his escort. Soon we were well acquainted. He became "Slim" to all of us.

We learned early of his liking for practical jokes. He was not above trying them in the air. Often when we made flights together, he in one pursuit plane and I in another, he would play around me, seeing how close he could fly his plane to mine without touching it. Sometimes he actually rubbed the wings of my ship.

In the winter of 1927-28 Lindbergh spent a great deal of time at Selfridge Field. It was on one of these visits that he proposed inaugurating a transcontinental passenger air line. And it was out of that quite serious proposition that came what I am sure must be the most effective practical joke he ever played in his life. I know what I am talking about, for he played the joke on me.

The corporation formed was called the Transcontinental Air Transport, Inc. Lindbergh refused to become an officer or a director in the company, but did accept a position as chairman of the Technical Committee of the organization. His salary was $10,000 a year.

In August of that year I resigned from the army to become vice-president of the new corporation and assistant to Lindbergh on the Technical Committee.

For some time we had considered a survey flight for this new airline. Colonel Breckinridge, Lindbergh and I were to make the first trip, using a cabin plane which was a sister ship to the Spirit of St. Louis, with seats for passengers in place of one of the large gas tanks.

One evening in New York, Lindbergh and I

were being entertained at a party. Slim left around midnight, but I decided to remain.

At about 3 A.M., not long after I had gone to bed, the telephone rang. It was Slim.

"I've decided to make that survey flight," he said. "I'll pick you up in thirty minutes."

I dragged myself sleepily out of bed and dressed. Half an hour later Slim arrived with Colonel Breckinridge and my luggage and we drove off for Roosevelt Field.

Take Off Before Dawn

It was still dark as we flew over Manhattan. We went first to Pittsburgh, then on to Columbus, Ohio. From there we headed for St. Louis.

Our plane had a cruising speed of 110 miles an hour and we were bucking a head wind all the way. When we got to St. Louis it was almost dark, and I was glad of it; I would get a chance to sleep.

Lindbergh, however, insisted that we proceed to Wichita, Kansas. We reached there about midnight, went to a hotel. I think I fell into bed.

It seemed I had scarcely closed my eyes when I was awakened by Slim.

"Time to take off for Los Angeles," he said.

I protested. But we were in the air again at four that morning. I'd had not quite four hours' sleep in the preceding forty-eight.

We reached Amarillo, Texas, and gassed, then headed immediately for the Rockies.

Lindbergh had told me, before we left Amarillo, that he had put extra large gas tanks in this ship. "She's good for nine hours at 1,750 r.p.m.s.," he said. That meant this ship could fly at cruising speed for nine hours before we'd need more gas.

We hit Gallup, New Mexico, opposite the Grand Canyon, in just about nine hours.

"Ever seen the Grand Canyon?" Slim asked me.

We had less than five minutes of flying left. Then we'd be out of fuel. I was worried.

"No," I said. "I've never seen the Grand Canyon. Listen, Slim. Is there a landing field here?"

"Don't worry about fields," he said. "I want to show you the canyon."

I began to argue. Only two minutes more, I told him, and we'd be out of gas. But he was stubborn. He banked to the left and headed toward the Grand Canyon.

It was fifteen minutes later that we flew out over the canyon. I know, because I was checking my watch and wondering how much longer our luck would hold. The sight nearly made me forget my worries. From the air it looked as though some Cyclopean monster with giant hands on a more giant plow had slowly turned a huge furrow in the desert rocks.

Now Lindbergh was diving below the level of the canyon's top.

"How do you like it?" he asked.

"It's swell, Slim," I replied. "But let's get out of here. If your motor ever conks, we're done."

"Nonsense!" he shouted.

Just then the motor started to miss—sure indication of a gas shortage. I looked at Slim. His face was serious. I wondered if I had been mistaken in my estimate of this famous pilot's skill and caution.

Slim the Joker

Suddenly the motor picked up. We began to climb. In a short time we were safely out of the canyon. We flew to Red Buttes, where we landed at an excellent field.

Slim was grinning broadly. I had suspicions.

"What's it all about?" I demanded.

"I forgot to tell you, back at Amarillo, that I've got a reserve of ten gallons of gas in the ship."

"Then why did the engine miss?"

"Oh," he explained, grinning, "I did that on purpose. Wanted to give you a thrill."

I had no answer. I was groggy from lack of sleep and in no mood for jokes. But that was Lindbergh's idea of a good one.

This, then, was Slim—the Lindbergh I knew in those carefree years immediately after he had made the epochal flight that elevated him, overnight, to the status of America's hero. A tall, gangling, blond-haired youth. A daring yet cautious pilot. Persistent and generous. Enough animal spirits to relish a practical joke from either the giving or receiving end.

I knew Slim then.

And I knew him later, when tragedy, swift and cruel as the blade of a prop, cleaved into his life.

But that is another story.

Howard Hughes~Record Breaker

by Rupert Hughes

Howard Hughes held the transcontinental speed record of nine hours 25 minutes when this photo was taken.

Popular author Rupert Hughes was Howard Hughes uncle, who knew things about his nephew Clifford Irving never dug up.

In view of the fact that Howard Hughes brought back to America the world's speed record for landplanes and in view of the editor's opinion that he is "the most picturesque young man in the country today," I have been invited to write his life story. This puts me in the two paradoxical positions of being the poor uncle of a rich nephew, and the biographer of one who, instead of being dead, is only half my own age. But what of it?

In a very real sense Howard was heavily handicapped from the day of his birth. Let me explain: The other day, at a meeting of a committee of the Will Rogers Memorial Commission, the question rose as to just what definition could be given to the term "handicapped children," since it had been agreed to devote the Rogers Memorial Fund to their welfare.

Our dear English language is so elastic that I said: "When you come right down to it, who is the most heavily handicapped person in any sport? It is the one who starts at scratch. They concede him all the so-called advantages and so they give all the real advantages to his rivals. And in daily life what could be a more dreadful handicap to any child than being the son of a rich and brilliant man?" Jesse H. Jones, the chairman of the Reconstruction Finance Corporation, heartily agreed:

"Take your own nephew, for example. I knew and loved your brother Howard for many years. When he died he left an only son hardly more than eighteen years old. That boy suddenly finds himself in complete control of a great factory and a great fortune built up slowly by a father who was one of the great men of his day. What further handicap could any young man have?"

Genius, they say, usually skips a generation; but Howard's genius is more like his father's

84

than that of any of his ancestors. His grandfathers on his mother's and father's side were both lawyers and both judges; and both families came from Kentucky, going thither from Virginia. The Ganos were of old Huguenot stock. When the first to arrive here fled from persecution and massacre in France, they settled at New Rochelle, New York, in the 1680s.

Howard's beautiful mother, Allene, was the daughter of Judge Gano, who was a direct descendant of the Rev. John Gano, the most famous chaplain in the Revolutionary War. The story persists that he converted George Washington to the Baptist faith and secretly baptized him. There are affidavits to support the family tradition.

I don't believe the story for a moment and I have no respect for affidavits; but there is far more historical evidence for the Gano legend than for the utterly unfounded and universally popular fable that George Washington left his comfortable headquartes at Valley Forge, went out to kneel in the snow, and prayed so vociferously that the Quaker Isaac Potts overheard him. There aren't even affidavits for that, and it was utterly unlike George Washington.

But Valley Forge is a long way from Houston, Texas, where young Howard Robard Hughes was born. He was a Christmas gift to his parents, arriving on December 24, 1905.

He was named after his father; consequently, the family name for him was, and still is, "Son."

Young Howard had, and has, the gift of finishing things, of throwing his whole soul and strength into the last crucial moment. His father had it. His grandfather had it. My father fought one lawsuit up and down the courts for twenty-six years. Then the United States Supreme Court gave a drastic decision against him. But he went right on, tried another line, and won the case anyway.

Young Howard's determination showed itself even in music. As a boy he took up the saxophone and drove his family almost insane with his tootlings; but he would not let it alone till he had mastered it. He took up motion pictures because they fascinated him, and made some of the biggest pictures ever turned out. His interest in aviation and years of flying led him to select for his *magnum opus* an airplane epic which he called Hell's Angels.

The World Almanac for 1936 did not mention his name, since it carried the aviation records only to August, 1935.

But in September Howard put himself at the head of the whole world of speed in landplanes. He did it twice in succession because he was too fast for the official timing cameras the first time.

From his earliest years he gave promise of high achievement. When he was about eleven or twelve I visited his father at Houston. Wireless telegraphy was a newer miracle then than now, but the boy had rigged up a wireless set in his own bedroom and spent his evenings picking up messages from ships in the Gulf of Mexico.

The Damned Thing Ran

A little later he was pleading in vain for a motorcycle. His parents would sooner have given him a buzz saw. But he had a bicycle—an ordinary nude bicycle. So he got himself a storage battery, connected it to an automobile self-starter motor which he bought at a junk yard, and attached that to his bicycle. And the damned thing ran.

After graduating from Thacher School he was under the minimum age for admission to the California Institute of Technology, but the dean, Dr. Robert Millikan, permitted him to take special courses without enrolling as a regular student.

My brother was so grateful that he asked Dr. Millikan if there were not something he could do to show his appreciation.

Dr. Millikan answered that the Institute had a fund from which loans were made to promising students who could not afford to pay their way through; but they always paid the money back, since fine jobs were always waiting for them the moment they left.

A larger fund would admit more promising young men to a sure career.

"How much would you want?" said my brother.

As he was writing the check, Dr. Millikan said:

"How shall we call this gift? The Howard R. Hughes Fund—or—or what?"

Howard answered:

"Unless you promise never to mention my name you don't get the check."

He got the check, and the young men for whom that money opened golden doors have never known who opened them.

The same dislike for publicity that characterized his father characterizes the son.

Perhaps a few words about his father would come in handy here to explain where Howard got his handicaps of money and encouragement, his mechanical skill and courage.

When my brother was born, his father was a young lawyer in the Missouri village of Lancaster. He was caught up in a desperate battle between rival groups of railroad builders, and he risked his life with the same calm fearlessness that later marked both Howards. In time a small railroad called my father to an attorneyship in Keokuk, Iowa, and he moved his family there. In time he became president of the railroad. When it was absorbed by the Burlington system, he returned to his law practice and became a judge.

A Restless Mechanical Genius

As a boy my brother Howard was restless and reckless, with a marked genius for mechanical things and a costly zest for taking watches, clocks, engines of every sort apart to see what made them go. He was not so skillful in putting things together again and our home was without a timepiece for many years. He was a wild boy, hopeless in the classroom and regular only in being expelled from every school he was sent to. Still, as our devoted mother indignantly declared: "Howard was never expelled from a school that was worthy of him." He was twenty before he decided to give up his ignorance. He secured tutors, went to Iowa State University, and then to Harvard.

But his mechanical mind drew him away from gentle pursuits.

He tried gold mining, silver mining, Mexico. He was engaged in lead and zinc mining near Joplin, Missouri, when the great oil field at Beaumont, Texas, began to send forth its record-breaking gushers. He dropped lead and hastened south for oil.

He had an uncanny gift for extracting money from my father for his wildest schemes and he was soon a leading oil man going from field

to field. One year he had fifty thousand in the bank. The next he owed the bank fifty thousand.

He went from Texas to Oklahoma to Louisiana. In one of his fields he and his partner, Walter Sharp, ran up against a barrier that was wrecking all the operators. There were vast deposits of oil down below, but they lay beneath a roof of flint that snapped off the fishtail bits at a ruinous rate. It took four days to make four inches of progress.

Finally Walter Sharp said:

"Howard, only a miracle can save us. You go home and put that brain of yours to inventing something to get us through."

So Howard took the train home. And by the time that he reached there he had an idea. As soon as the family greetings were over he called for a breadboard from the kitchen, fastened paper on it, and, sitting at the dining-room table, began to sketch his model. He emerged from the family dining room with an Archimedean cry of "Eureka!" and the picture of a bit that had no less than 166 cutting edges!

He took the first train for Springfield, Massachusetts, where he showed his drawings to a big firm that manufactured models for such inventions. The heads of the firm said:

"It's mighty pretty but it won't work. If it did cut the rock you couldn't keep it oiled a thousand feet or so underground. We like money but we don't want to take yours for such an impossible dream."

"Make it anyway," said Howard.

The Bit That Shouldn't Work

When at last it was finished they offered to show him why it wouldn't work. They set a big block of granite on a trestle, fixed the bit to a rod, and said:

"When we start the conveyer belt going you'll see that your bit won't bite. It will just go round and round on the surface."

Howard nodded grimly and they started the thing to whirling. Before they could stop the belt, the bit had gone through six feet of granite, dropped to the floor, and was burrowing through the solid concrete as if it were cake.

So Howard hurried south to the oil field and set his bit to work on that flint barrier. It loved flint and went through it at such unheard-of speed that all the other operators screamed for the Hughes conical bit. He couldn't manufacture it fast enough. He rented the bits on royalty. The demand came from all around the globe.

His factory grew and grew till it was one of the largest in the South. The bit, in one adaptation or another, took everything in stride, and all the nations clamored for it. It is a very pretty thing to see: something like three cones working together and simply chewing the bewildered rock to shreds.

The Encylcopedia Britannica in its twelfth edition published a picture of it as the last word in mining. The editors of the Dictionary of American Biography felt that Howard deserved a niche among our immortals.

Orphaned Heir at Eighteen

All this time, of course, young Howard was only a boy, though he took a precocious interest in all his father's manifold inventions and improvements in various fields. Howard was destined to lose both his mother and father in his youth in a little less than two years. It was while the boy was at the Thacher School, Ojai, California, in March, 1922, that I received one night a heartbroken telegram from my brother, saying that Allene, his wife, had died suddenly. He had telegraphed young Howard at Ojai, telling him merely that his mother was ill and he had better come home. My brother asked me to meet the boy when he came down from Ojai and put him on the first train for Texas.

Young Howard, then just sixteen, arrived in great anxiety and suspense. I hesitated a long while over telling him the bitter truth. My poor brother, I knew, had suffered so much in the death of his beloved and beautiful wife that telling his son the news would be too much to put upon him. So I steeled myself, told young Howard the truth, and tried to uphold him in his first great tragedy.

He was in Houston at the time of his father's death, but I had to break the hearts of my own father and mother with word of their loss. Soon after the funeral young Howard came out to Los Angeles to be with his disconsolate grandparents, and lived at my house. He had just turned eighteen by two weeks.

He found himself in control of a great fac-

tory and of a large fortune, part of which he decided to invest in motion pictures.

For his interest in the movies I was partly to blame, though unintentionally. At that time I was also a victim of the same infatuation. I was directing pictures of my own writing, and young Howard spent hours on the set, in the projection room, in listening to story conferences and studying the entire business with insatiable interest.

It is a fascinating life at best, or worst; and soon after his father's death Howard plunged into it. He had come under the spell of the electrically vivacious Marshall Neilan, director of many very successful pictures. He had a promising idea for a picture but no idea where to get the money for it. Howard put up the

Howard dated many of Hollywood's top starlets, among them Ida Lupino.

cash, and the picture, Everybody's Acting, issued in 1926, made money. According to one authority, it paid fifty per cent profit.

This naturally stimulated Howard's interest. Together with John Considine, he set to work on an elaborate melodramatic comedy called Two Arabian Knights. They engaged as their director the forceful and intelligent Lewis Milestone, who was born in Russia, educated in Belgium, and re-educated in the cutting rooms of Hollywood studios, where he worked for several years before John and Howard gave him his first opportunity. For the two knights they engaged Louis Wolheim and William Boyd. The result was an exciting and amusing picture well made and well received.

Boy Producer

It lured Howard deeper into the jungle. He took up production on his own with his own organization, which he called the Caddo Company, as a tribute to the Caddo oil fields in Louisiana, which had been very good to his father. More or less to Howard's own surprise, he was gradually dragged into a gigantic production that swept the world as the most spectacular picture of its time.

According to the legend, Marshall Neilan had an idea for a picture concerning war aviation, and Howard, shaking off all dependence on others, bought the plot and began to write the scenario himself, with the able assistance of Harry Behn, who had been connected with The Big Parade and other famous pictures.

In the first plans for the picture, Howard is said to have estimated the cost at a modest six hundred thousand. The movies had gone a long way from the dark ages of 1903, when the producers of the first successful story picture, The Great Train Robbery, were laughed at as liars because they pretended to have spent four hundred dollars on it and taken several days in the shooting. It ran eight hundred feet in the finished version and it was said that several hundred feet were shot that were not used.

He had put Lewis Milestone under a long-term contract as a director, but Two Arabian Knights brought Milestone a great reputation and Howard did not wish to divide the credit for Hell's Angels with any one. He borrowed Luther Reed from Paramount studios. But Reed, who had been an aviation editor for the New York Herald and knew the air, had ideas of his own, and friction developed to such a point that one day, after an earnest talk, Reed resigned and Howard announced that he would direct the picture himself.

For his male stars Howard had secured the loan of James Hall and Ben Lyon. They resented the direction of the inexperienced producer and objected to his telling them how to play their scenes. Howard says that "they were justified in that feeling."

Gradually the two leading men and the young director came to an understanding. The original leading woman of the picture was lost on the way. The Norwegian beauty Greta Nissen had been enaged. She lasted through the first version of the picture—a silent version that was completed just as the talking picture struck the motion-picture world like a thunderbolt, wrecking countless properties, personalities, and reputations, and toppling even popular idols like John Gilbert into oblivion or worse.

The motion-picture companies had to make an immediate outlay of countless millions of dollars for new studio and theater equipment and experimentation—this on top of a private panic in the business that preceded the cataclysm of 1929 by several years.

But none of the fortunetellers who fatten on movie money foretold this double panic, and Howard had no warning of what lay ahead of him when the first camera was turned October 31, 1927. He had sufficient troubles as it was when he proceeded to make his epic as a silent drama.

By the time Howard had finished all of his picture except the airplane shots, he had spent over three hundred thousand dollars. Now he built a miniature city of London for the Zepelin to attack. Next he gathered together a fleet of forty planes of all sorts for battles in the air. The cost of this made a pretty total.

Even in the pursuit of beauty there was immense expense. Howard knew that, in some of his celestial scenes, clouds were necessary for drama. The generally cloudless skies of California have their advantages for lovers of fair weather, but they make a monotonous background for planes and destroy the effect of

Howard Hughes dominated any group. Here he is shown with a group of reporters at lunch.

motion, the airships often looking as if they hung from strings.

Howard wanted clouds. He wanted great masses of them to give the battle drama; for his men were fighting among the cloud gods as did the great hammer god Thor.

But the clouds would not come at his beck and call. They would not form till he gave up. Then they would muster en masse, only to vanish before his lenses. In his planes he could chase them for leagues. His scouts would telephone that there were mountains of cloud over Long Beach. He would dart thither with his planes and his cameras in planes. The clouds would roll away. He left southern California for northern, and there he secured majestic backgrounds.

According to the reports, Hell's Angels had now cost Howard three million dollars. It is certain that it had taken up a year and a half of his time. After months of preparation he had given the signal for the first camera to start rolling on October 31, 1927. The first projection machine at the first preview spilled the picture before the first audience in March, 1929.

It was a silent picture, and the audience received it in silence. The public had turned against the silent drama almost overnight.

Such a preview is one of fervent suspense for all concerned in any case. Howard's high hopes went into a tail spin and crashed because the audience was puzzled by the incongruous pantomime of the actors and the old-fashioned printed titles. Planes zoomed and cannon fired, people talked and shouted, blazing planes smote the earth; but never a sound was heard. Howard's film was mute and the audience might as well have been deaf.

There was nothing for Howard to do but give it sound. This meant reshooting everything but the aerial material. The uproar of that could be added to the sound track.

The problem of revision meant much more than merely adding spoken dialogue. The whole story must be retold for the ear as well as the eye.

The picture was not ready for release as a talkie until May, 1930, when it opened at Grauman's Chinese Theater in Hollywood. The first camera had turned on the silent version October 31, 1927. Howard had spent more than two years on it. According to the newspapers, it had cost him four million dollars. It actually cost him a little over two million.

There was great curiosity over the picture and for the opening night all the tickets were

89

sold a week in advance at eleven dollars a seat. Speculators sold some at fifty dollars apiece.

Its success was instantaneous, gigantic. The public flocked to it, the critics flung superlatives at it: "It stands alone as the greatest of air pictures." "The most beautiful shots and thrilling action the movies have yet built." "Beside its sheer magnificence all stage spectacles and colossal circuses become puny."

He sent it across to England with some trepidation, but the critics there were even more rapturous. The London Times said that it had "no equal on the screen." The Daily Express said it was "the greatest masterpiece the screen has ever known."

This was pretty good for a young man of twenty-four!

Movies to Mystery Ship

Hell's Angels was not his only picture, big as it was. During its production he also produced Racket and The Mating Call, both with Thomas Meighan in the star parts. In the year following completion of Hell's Angels he produced five more: 'The Age for Love, Cock of the Air, Sky Devils, The Front Page, and Scarface. The Front Page brought Pat O'Brien to the screen. Scarface gave Paul Muni his first screen opportunity. Howard also contributed to the films George Raft, Ann Dvorak, Karen Morley, and Louis Wolheim.

After making five pictures in one year he decided that he had enough of motion pictures for the time being.

But this was not a mere whimsical dropping of a toy. He had mastered the field and made several good pictures, including one of the greatest ever made. He saw before him a more tempting field of conquest. He was not yet quite so old as Alexander the Great when he wept because he had no more worlds to conquer.

What the witch burners and wizard hangers would do to our aviators if they came into power again makes one shudder almost as much as the feats of the sky piercers. In days not so far back the sun and the planets were supposed to be only thirty-five miles overhead—only a little farther than our stratosphere baloonists have probed. A century ago people figured that if a railroad train went twenty miles an hour

all the passengers would go blind from watching the landscape. And now people hardly look up when an almost invisible plane writes advertisements in almost infinite letters across the blue manuscript pages of heaven.

About three years ago Howard engaged a few young graduates of engineering school. Under the supervision of two very brilliant men, Dick Palmer and Glen Odekirk, he put them to work in the back of an old hangar at Glendale, California.

The place was well guarded and so were the drawings that poured from it into a blueprint shop.

In time six more men were hired, wood- and metalworkers and mechanics. For eighteen months their doings were kept secret, though Howard's connection with them, and the task at which they were engaged had become known. It was called the mystery ship.

In August, 1935, an aviation magazine said of it: "Hughes' ship is still a mystery. No dope on its design, construction, or performance has been released. The wings are of combined wood and metal construction. The rest of the ship is all metal. Both the landing gear and the tail wheel are retractable. Wind-tunnel tests are supposed to have indicated a possible speed of 365 m. p. h."

On August 18, 1935, he was ready for the preliminary test hop. He took his "mystery ship" to the Municipal Airport of Los Angeles and ran almost the length of the field for his takeoff.

New Speed Record

This delayed take-off was due to the fact that, in order to cut down air resistance and gain speed, the wings had been made very small. The ratio of the plane's weight to its wing area was about twice the normal. This meant that every square foot of wing had to lift twice the usual load. Consequently the ship had to take a long run to build up a speed at which the wings would lift it from the ground.

Once aloft, Howard flew in a leisurely circle for about a quarter of an hour, then brought the ship down and landed it.

On September 12, 1935, he appeared at the Martin Field near Santa Ana, California, for an attempt against the world speed record. It

Howard Hughes designed this "Racer" plane at a cost of $100,000.

was here that Dr. Albert A. Michelson had established the speed of light at 186,000 miles a second. All the conditions established by the National Aeronautic Association and the Fédération Aeronautique Internationale were complied with. Cameras were set up and the course measured at 3 kilometers, or 1.86 miles, and an electric timing device installed.

The judges who watched from an observation plane were Amelia Earhart Putnam, the pilot Paul Mantz, and Lawrence Therkelson, official of the N. A. A. There were other officials on the ground.

It was late in the afternoon before everything was ready, and though it was the 12th of the month, the flight began as it ended with the bad luck ordinarily associated with the 13th. First, Howard cruised over the course for a while at a mere 302 miles an hour; then entered it again on a dive from the sky, which was ruled as a disqualification, though he was clocked at 346 m.p.h. He banked, came back for a second try, and reached 352 m.p.h. He tried it again and made 339 m.p.h.; but it was now so dusky that the cameras failed to catch him. The judges ruled that four consecutive runs across the course properly made and clocked were necessary before the record could be called official.

The best previous record had been made by the French ace Delmotte in a plane on which the French government is said to have spent a million dollars. His speed of 314.319 miles an hour on December 26, 1934, had taken the crown away from the late James Wedell.

The next morning, the 13th, Howard was on hand again, and conformed to all the regulations while the timing device and the cameras were doing their duty to the satisfaction of the officials.

The official tests were finished, but Howard decided to make an extra run over the course with the engine wide open. Just as he entered the course at a terrific speed, the motor cut out. He shut off the gasoline tank, which had failed to feed, and turned on another tank. However, the motor refused to run again, in spite of the fact there was plenty of gasoline in both tanks. He could not get back to the airport, and there was only a beet field in front of him. As he was about to lower his retracted landing gear, he realized that if he did he would be carried across a concrete highway and probably wreck the plane and perhaps himself. He was inspired to set his ship down on her belly at a hundred-miles-an-hour clip. She skidded along the soft ground to an eventual halt, with only a propeller bent and the cowling dented. By the time the anxious spectators arrived they found Howard calmly seated on the propeller hub.

In due course of time his record was established as authentic by the American and International Associations and the mark set at 352.388 m.p.h. Howard says that the plane is capable of 385 m.p.h. During the first of his runs across the course, the covering over the cockpit blew off and this opening slowed the plane about 15 m.p.h. Also, he had used only 900 of the 1,100 horsepower now available.

MEMOIRS AND MEMORIES

General Douglas MacArthur was the military man supreme, handsome fighting hero, legend in his own time, credit to his country. Son of a Civil War hero and a fiercely ambitious mother, MacArthur basked in the adulation of the public from World War I to Korea. At the time this article was written, the super-general appeared destined for the shadows of oblivion. But with the advent of World War II, he turned out to be the necessary man in the proper place at the right time. Later, in Korea, his tactics earned some disapproval and he became a figure of top-level controversy, but nothing ever altered his fierce personal pride or his four-star showmanship. The name MacArthur will always appear in history books and that's how the General—not to mention his mother—wanted it.

MacArthur's biographer in the following article was Drew Pearson, the Washington journalist who became almost as famous as the General. Pearson hit national headlines early in the Thirties with a gossipy book called Washington Merry-Go-Round, written with Robert S. Allen. Eventually, Pearson lost his partner and wrote a column on his own—the one now conducted by Jack Anderson, who for years was Pearson's aide. Like MacArthur, Pearson was respected and feared by colleagues.

The Barrymores were the Royal Family of the American Theatre. Ethel, the only girl, was so beautiful as a young actress that Winston Churchill among others fell in love with her. Yet the stage was this girl's true love, as it was with her brothers Lionel and John. Not until the early Thirties did Ethel appear on the screen, and then the three Barrymores appeared in the successful Rasputin and the Empress. From then on, Ethel alternated between stage and screen. You may recall her deep, throaty tones from various sound tracks.

This article was written well before her Hollywood days. Yet her feelings for the stage never changed.

The Real General MacArthur

by Drew Pearson and Robert S. Allen

In 1942, General Douglas MacArthur was residing somewhere in the South Pacific diligently engaged in defeating the armies of the Japanese Empire. In the United States, his fame and recognition as one of the leading military minds of this century was already established.

Columnists Drew Pearson and Robert Allen succeeded in capturing some of the more interesting details of the general's life in the following article.

As the fierce battle around Manila neared climax, an old army friend of General Douglas MacArthur remarked, "Doug may have to swim for it, and he can still do it. But he'll have to leave his medals behind."

At sixty-two MacArthur is stronger than most men at fifty, but his array of medals, the visible tokens of a long, brilliant career would sink him. They include the D.S.C., the D.S.M., the Purple Heart (all with oak-leaf cluster), the Silver Star with six oak-leaf clusters, Grand Officer Legion of Honor, Croix de Guerre with three palms, and so on down the line. Total estimated weight, sixteen pounds, thirteen ounces.

Those who know Douglas MacArthur are not surprised at his brilliant performance in the Philippines. His whole life is one long glitter of brilliance.

He was even born brilliantly. His father was General Arthur MacArthur, who at the age of seventeen enlisted in the Union Army, became "the boy colonel of the West," who led his troops in a dashing charge up Missionary Ridge. In his later years the father again achieved fame for cleaning up the Philippines.

To his brilliant birth, record at West Point, and in World War I, MacArthur also added a brilliant marriage. He married a daughter of the Philadelphia Stotesburys.

It was while MacArthur was serving his tour of duty as Commander of the Philippine Department that news of his divorce reached Manila. A group of Filipino newspapermen came out to the General's headquarters and asked whether he would object to publication of the story. They would suppress it if he desired.

"No," replied MacArthur; "put it on the front page if you want to."

Ruler of the Philippines

This increased his popularity with the Filipinos, already at a high pitch. Throughout the governorship of Henry L. Stimson, the Filipinos ran to MacArthur with their troubles, until when Dwight F. Davis came over as governor general, they had come to look upon MacArthur as the real ruler of the islands. Davis was deliberate, taking days to come to a decision. MacArthur became more and more disgusted with him, and after a while was say-

MacArthur with his aides in France during the first World War.

ing, more or less publicly, that he didn't like Davis and didn't care if Davis knew it.

MacArthur's great popularity with the Filipinos was to serve him in good stead when, in 1936, he returned as Field Marshal of the Philippine Army.

MacArthur has never lacked dramatic color at any turn of the road. In World War I the Rainbow Division was his idea, a division made up of men from every state in the Union. He served as a brigade commander in, and later as commander of, that heroic division. His personal record in action was as brilliant as the rest of his career. He was wounded twice, gassed once, and was decorated by a dozen foreign governments.

Carrying nothing but a swagger stick and always wearing an officer's cap with the stiffening wire pulled out, MacArthur was continually in the front-line trenches. His appearance made him readily distinguishable from the enemy lines, and his carelessness is exposing himself unquestionably detracted from his usefulness as a general officer. But it had inspiring effect on his troops.

MacArthur's bravery was foolhardy but colorful. On one occasion, when he wanted some information about the enemy which no one had supplied, he went over the top himself, took a German dugout by surprise, and came back with a couple of prisoners.

MacArthur had advanced from a major to brigadier general during the war, and he was the only brigadier below the permanent rank of colonel to keep his temporary rank afterward. Later Congress passed a law requiring that future promotions to brigadier general be made only from the rolls of colonels. But it was significant that this was done after MacArthur got his star. Since then MacArthur has twice been a full general—once as Chief of Staff (at the age of fifty; the youngest man ever to reach that post, which he also held longer than any other incumbent); and now again by special act of the President last December. Today MacArthur wears the four stars as Commander of the United States Armed Forces in the Far East.

There are few in the country today who would not be willing to give MacArthur a decoration of any dimension he might name as an award of honor for his heroic defense of the Philippines. But a few years back it was different.

As Chief of Staff, MacArthur was a hero to the Regular Army because of his determined battle against the senseless economics of the Hoover regime. The present Chief of Staff, General George C. Marshall, says with a wry smile, "We used to have all the time and none of the money; now we have plenty of money and no time." When MacArthur was Chief of Staff he knew what those words meant: he had time but no money. The big struggle throughout his term as Chief of Staff was against economy cuts.

One-Man Crusade

Roosevelt succeeded Hoover and the Budget Bureau proposed a cut in the War Department appropriation in the spring of 1933. MacArthur waged a one-man crusade against any reductions. Summoned by Lewis Douglas, Budget Director and wielder of the President's pruning knife, MacArthur stalled the cut by saying he needed time to study the matter.

Several weeks passed. MacArthur returned and flatly refused to make the requested reductions. A few days later he was summoned to the White House. There the President personally directed his Chief of Staff to comply

"I have returned"

95

with the necessary economies. MacArthur again asked for time to make another "study."

His defiance was so serious that rumors began to circulate that he would be replaced by a Chief of Staff more sympathetic with the administration's viewpoint. But, though MacArthur lost that particular fight, he remained in office throughout his term and longer; and all during the time he, more than the late Secretary of War Dern, fought against cuts in the army appropriation.

When MacArthur took over the job of building up the defenses of the Philippines in 1935, with the title of Field Marshal and a salary of $18,000 a year, not counting his luxurious air-conditioned penthouse apartment atop a Manila hotel, he was again confronted with the battle of getting money for men and guns. President Quezon was lavish one day, frugal the next. Few people in the United States cared whether or not MacArthur succeeded. He had been kicked upstairs, they thought, to a romantic job in the South Seas with a fat salary and a high-sounding title. It was all that any man could expect—and better than most retired officers ever got.

Except for an occasional derisive thrust, MacArthur and his Philippines were rapidly forgotten. The fact is, he had little at that time to command much attention. He was not commander of the American forces in the Philippines, as he is today. He was merely a hired officer in charge of a band of ill-trained Filipinos. The American soldiers in the Philippines were under the command of United States officers.

Furthermore, for all his high-sounding title, MacArthur was the object of every conceivable opposition to his defense program. He had been promised a military budget of $8,000,000 a year, but by the time the Filipino politicians got through lobbying for pork-barrel projects and the Japanese fifth columnists got through doing their slick dirty work, MacArthur's budget was cut to the bone.

Despite these heartbreaking obstacles, MacArthur doggedly persisted on the unswerving thesis that the Philippines could be defended. For years military experts had contended this could not be done. MacArthur flatly asserted it could, and made all his plans and preparations accordingly.

Today he has a new title, but his thesis is the same. On July 26, 1941, President Roosevelt made MacArthur Commanding General of the United States Armed Forces in the Far East, thereby making him C.O. not only of the Philippine army of 125,000 soldiers, but also of the United States armed forces in the Philippines. The President's action was far from merely a personal tribute to Douglas MacArthur. It was an official declaration to the world that the United States government regarded the Philippines as something more than a sugar colony preparing for independence. The strategic islands became a military outpost which this government intends to fight for to the last ditch.

Thus by one stroke the full might of the United States was placed behind the thesis which for six years has been advocated with few listeners by Douglas MacArthur.

With this long delayed official recognition of his theory came, also overdue, a loosening of purse strings. Men and materiel in great quantities were rushed to the Philippines. But by the end of 1941 it was not only Untied States soldiers and munitions that were moving into the islands. The Japs, too, were pouring in.

Luzon, Corregidor, Mindanao—strange names flashed into the headlines. The attack began the same day as Pearl Harbor, and every day since then the name MacArthur has appeared on the front page of every paper in the land. Mary MacArthur would have been very happy had she lived to see it. Her son had risen to the stature of a national hero for whom thousands nightly pray on bended knee.

Backstage

by Ethel Barrymore

Ethel Barrymore, stage star and mother, with her three children.

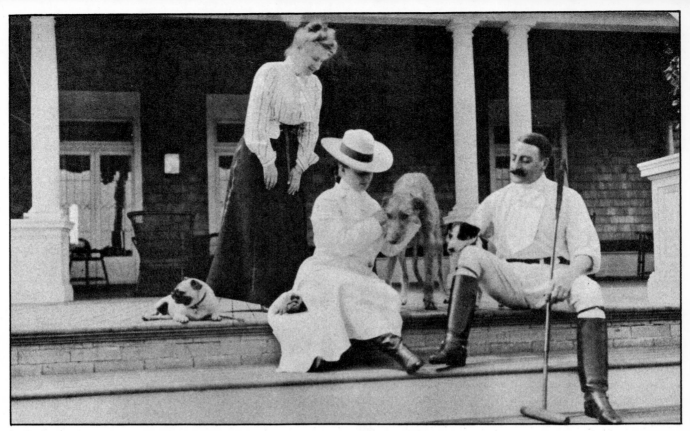

Ethel Barrymore was a member of a stage family. With her, John Drew, her famous acting uncle.

Ethel Barrymore, First Lady of the American Theatre, wrote this in 1926, when she was best known as a Broadway actress.

We lived in terms of theatrical dialogue. Even grandmother's house at No. 140 North Twelfth Street, Philadelphia, was known to us as the Tomb of the Capulets. I can recall now how very large it seemed, with tremendous cavelike rooms and cavernous halls filled with most terrifying echoes. It always frightened me a little because I felt so tiny.

Of my memory treasures of those days the greatest, I think, is my recollection of Madame Madjeska, to me a veritable fairy queen. I loved her for herself, but her devotion to my mother tinged that affection with reverence. It was she who so convinced my mother that we all joined the Catholic Church. Madame Modjeska herself served as Lionel's godmother and her husband, Count Bozenta Chlapowski, sponsored me.

To the Drews and my father, devout Episcopalians, this conversion was an amusing shock. But mother was most sincere and rigorously lived up to all of the demands of the Church. And that observance brought about one of the most picturesque "scenes" between my mother and father I ever witnessed.

One Saturday morning as mother was about to leave the house for early mass, she met my father just coming in. His opera cape was thrown jauntily back and his silk hat was slightly atilt. There was a rakish angle to the straight stick thrust beneath one arm. He greeted mother with a quizzical smile, a large gesture, and passed on, calling over his shoulder, "Go to mass, my dear."

Go To Hell, My Dear

Mother's smile was as quizzical, her gesture as copious as she replied, "Go to hell, my dear," and they went their separate ways. She was the gayest and most interesting person I ever have known. She was always radiant, always happy, with an amazing reserve of good spirits. She was ever witty—indeed, it was impossible for her to be otherwise—and her banter flashed like sun on bright steel. This vast good humor was a characteristic of the Drews.

In the midst of her active career on the stage my mother cared for her children without a thought that the much mooted question of career and motherhood might apply to her.

When anyone asks me if a married woman can have a career I can only recite the history of my family. My grandmother had four children and a career and my mother had three children and a career. I have three children. Mrs. John Drew, mother of my uncle, had a theater in Philadelphia which she managed for fifty years. In addition to her domestic duties she succeeded in presenting the foremost actors of the time—Booth, Macready, McCullough—in that city. She went on the stage when she was three and was still active at seventy-eight, when she died.

Nor were we "trained" for the stage. It was about us, with us, part of us, so that unconsciously we absorbed it. As a matter of fact I was so bashful as a youngster that I suffered much in the classroom. Whenever I was called upon to recite I blushed. If I had to leave my seat and go to the blackboard it was like a "first night" to me. I had my full share of torture in this respect.

The ease with which other children glibly rattled off Shakespeare was a constant source of wonderment to me. The confidence of the amateur was not mine. I was always painfully self-conscious. Up to the time I went on the stage I showed no whit of aptitude for acting.

As for the claims of heredity no one could have told then what I might be. I remember that as children we used to act plays—but all children do that. And in my case it did not go deeper than mere play.

A Musical Career?

If the real truth were known it was confidently expected that I would accomplish great things with my music. Most of my schooldays were centered on the piano. I was given a medal when I was nine for playing a Beethoven sonata. In a general way my father knew what his daughter was "taking" at the convent, but how well it was taking did not dawn upon him until he came upon me playing Beethoven. He stood by spellbound. And as I looked up when I was through I could see that he was crying.

But I did very little with my music. My whole life has been concerned with the theater, my childhood was spent in it. Why, mother used to have us children in a basket in her dressing-room! We all have been part of the theater and I believe I am prouder of having fulfilled the traditions of my family than I am of anything else in the world. One of the best things in the world, I think, is to live according to the way you plan for yourself when you are young.

I cannot say that it is altogether heredity that took me into the theater. I suppose there is something in heredity, but looking back over my own life, it seems to me that it is the recollection of my mother and grandmother, of their work, of their struggles, of the hardships they endured, of their standards of sucess, that has led me on to effort.

It is my knowledge of what they were striving for that makes me feel that it is right for me to keep up my work on the stage. It is not my home life that has broadened my work, for I myself believe that my work is absolutely outside my home life. I do not believe that motherhood has anything whatever to do with an artist's expression. Expression in any art is a gift which grows with experience, with knowledge of life. The more you know of people, of their desires, of their ambitions, their mannerisms, the wider becomes the expression of your art.

Information is the artist's need. The more an actor knows of things, of people, of life, the better artist he is. As soon as he begins to lose interest in the whole of life, he begins to deteriorate as an artist. So many women seem to care nothing for information that I wonder how they spend their days. They sit soggily, heavily, looking out upon the world with uninterested eyes, while before them spreads the great panorama of life. Like the Lady of Shalott they look in the mirror while the cavalcade goes past on the highway.

Portray Life In Our Time

"To see life steadily and see it whole," you must know all men, all women, in their relations to the big scheme of things, and portray them with a skill that you have learned first from the gift within you, then from your years of work for the sake of that gift. Because I believe this I have always wanted to play roles that come closest to the life of today, to the

A young Ethel Barrymore as pictured in her Beverly Hills garden.

life that I know; roles that throb with the great problems of the women of today. If we want to use the stage as a mirror to display some dim figure of a dimmer past, that is our business. But I believe that our privilege is the portrayal of the life we can best depict, the life of our own time.

Women have never had such richness of expression, such power of growth as they have today. I believe that any woman artist, on the stage or elsewhere, is shirking her duty if she fails to show in her art that she is in touch with the fuller life of women.

Women are getting away from the faults of their training and coming in touch with the great issues of modernity with an enthusiasm that will react upon their development more intensely than men's ordinary interest in affairs now does. Women are branching out into the new lines of art; women are succeeding better in the old branches. Women are thinking, feeling, growing with a rapidity unparalleled in their history.

They realize the tremendously worth-while things that can be accomplished through this new growth, this ability to give something of value in partnerships. That largely explains my appearance with Mr. Hampden. When it was announced that Mr. Hampden and I were to appear together many of my friends inquired

why I purposed such an alliance even with so eminent an actor as Mr. Hampden.

The explanation is simple: I became associated with Mr. Hampden because it offered an opportunity I should not otherwise have of acting several great roles it always has been my desire to portray.

A woman has little chance in Shakespeare unless associated with a commanding actor. Hamlet never was produced for the sake of *Ophelia* alone, nor The Merchant of Venice for *Portia*, nor The Shrew for *Katharina*, nor Much Ado About Nothing for *Beatrice*, nor Macbeth for *Lady Macbeth*, great as all these roles are in their different ways.

As I wanted to play some of these parts and others it was necessary that I become allied with an actor of the needful artistic stature and versatility to portray the men and supermen of classic drama. In Mr. Hampden I found not only such an actor but also a producer and stage director rarely qualified by ideals and training to present the great plays in a manner worthy of themselves and their traditions.

And I think I can say with sincerity that this is a matter which works both ways. The fine actor needs a competent feminine opposite in Shakespearean drama if the best results are to be obtained. How well the public appreciates combinations of this kind has been shown by the illustrious careers of Henry Irving and Ellen Terry and of E. H. Sothern and Julie Marlowe.

Some have asked why I went outside my own family to form such an association. Why not play *Ophelia* to my brother John's *Hamlet*, or *Desdemona* to Lionel's *Othello*?

Some years ago it was even rumored that we intended doing this—a Hamlet production in which Lionel would be the *King* with John and me; and an Othello with John as *Iago* to Lionel's *Othello* and my *Desdemona*.

Really, the idea is absurd. We never contemplated such a thing. Impassioned scenes of love and jealousy such as this would demand would never be accepted from brother and sister. As greatly as I would like to appear in a cast with my brothers it would be asking too much from intelligent patrons of the theater—and from the actors.

PEOPLE AND PERSONALITIES

Mankind is in trouble, says Albert Einstein, the high-domed scholar-philosopher-scientist who by evoking the Theory of Relativity gave the world of the Twenties something to talk about, if not understand. With the rise of Hitler, the bushy haired Einstein came to this country and lived out his life as an illustrious exile, a warm if absent-minded human being who relaxed by playing the violin.

Einstein believed that, though we are in trouble, it may not be our fault. Perhaps the turbulent times are at fault. We are all decent human beings, he thinks, and we should join hands to work for the common good. But can this be done in the tempestuous Twentieth Century? That is his question . . .

Albert Einstein took a serious view of life. Not so James J. Walker, the most flamboyant Mayor in the exciting saga of New York City. In the Twenties when Jimmy Walker went abroad on a pleasure trip, the European press called him "Jazz" J. Walker, something our newspapers should have thought up first. Jazz J. thoroughly understood politics, but believed showmanship helped an ambitious man more. With the gift of showmanship a man could rise high on the ladder of success. Without it, he was sunk. In the following pages Jimmy, writing as a wiser man in the year 1939, assays the showmanship rating of men like Franklin D. Roosevelt, Fiorello H. La Guardia, and a few prominent Europeans.

Jimmy Walker was a personal showman, doing it all for number one. Walt Disney devoted his sense of showmanship, along with his genius for creativity, to cartoon characters like Mickey Mouse, Donald Duck, and Snow White. Success was not easy for this farm boy who loved animals from the start. But his wife was present when needed, and their determination won. In the Thirties, Donald Duck was as famous as the President of the United States. The laughter he and other Disney characters evoked was heard around the world.

He Gave Us MICKEY

by Jack Jamison

Jack Jamison wrote this article when Disney was just on the threshold of fame.

There is a young man, in Hollywood of all places, who could be a millionaire if he liked, but who smiles and shrugs and says, "No; I'm having too much fun this way, thanks."

He is Walt Disney, creator of Mickey Mouse.

In 1919 a young Red Cross ambulance driver came home from France to Kansas City, Missouri. He became a ten-dollar-a-week apprentice in a commercial art firm. Let out when business was slow, he carried mail for Uncle Sam, and shortly teamed up with another youngster who liked pencils and paper. They drew pictures of oil wells.

"The firm that was selling the oil wells told us to draw them the way they would look when the oil came in," Walter recollects. "You should have seen the amount of oil we got into those drawings!"

Always interested in cartoons, he next experimented with a motion-picture cartoon reel for a Kansas City chain of theaters, depicting local happenings and personalities. Finding that he had a knack for it, he laid out a series of fairy-tale cartoon reels to be shown in schools and churches. His backers failed, and he found himself reduced in assets to a pair of trousers, a sweater, a motion-picture camera, and a pair of shoes bought with five dollars borrowed from a friend; those, and a great faith in the possibilities of motion pictures.

Hollywood was motion-picture headquarters. Always impetuous, he sold the camera and arrived there with $40 to spare. His brother Roy was in Hollywood selling vacuum cleaners. He had $250 in a savings account.

Walter talked fast, and a few hours later Roy discovered himself to be in the motion-picture business. Walter's initial idea was to hire a child actress and let her act in the cartoons along with the drawn figures. For the first reel he did all the drawings himself—fifteen hundred of them. Its entertainment value was instantly recognized, and a studio gave him a contract to do a series.

"Success!" thought Walter, and promptly expanded his staff, hiring a young lady to help him ink in his drawings. She was an exceedingly pretty girl—and, as day after day they bent their heads together over a drawing board, Walter became increasingly aware of the fact. The upshot was inevitable, because she had as much faith in his cartoons as he had. In short, he married her.

Soon other people had to be hired, for Universal Studios invited the budding young concern to manufacture a cartoon having to do with a rabbit named Oswald. Walter thought rabbits were too meek and not up to enough devilment, but he made twenty-six Oswalds. The trouble, the studio found, was that he was always trying out new ideas and gadgets, wanting to spend money instead of just settle down into a rut and make it. They allowed his contract to lapse. He was in New York when he got the news, and his first thought was for the twenty young fellows out in Hollywood now working for him. He couldn't bear to let them know that they were out of jobs. With Mrs. Disney, he caught the first train for Hollywood, and on the train he wrote the scenario for the first feature production of Walt Disney Studios, Ltd.

The hero, he decided, would be a mouse. Mice were little and cute, and always up to mischief.

Of course he had no backing. But that was nothing.

The first Mickey Mouse reel was produced in a cramped room over the Disney garage. It had approximately one chance in a thousand of succeeding. Talkies had come in. Walter offered that tin can of celluloid to every studio in town. Not one of them showed interest in it. A year later every one of them was to bid frantically for it, but at the moment all they were interested in was bringing vaudeville acts to the screen. Anybody else would have been discouraged. Walt wasn't. He was having fun. Finally he located an independent producer who, in a flight of wild daring, agreed to risk a few dollars on the mouse. And that is how Mickey, born in an attic, first saw the light of the projection-machine arc lamps.

A few days before I last saw Walt Disney he happened by chance to run into the studio executive who let his contract run out because he "wasted the studio's money to have fun." They shook hands, and a deep silence fell. Finally, with a groan, the executive shook his head. "And I let you get away from me!" he commented.

For Mickey, today, is the most popular film star in the world. This is not exaggeration but the literal truth. Whether as Miki Kuchi in Japan or Mikkel Mus in Denmark, he lays honest claim to more enthusiastic fans than Greta Garbo, Clark Gable, and Marie Dressler put together. More than a million American youngsters belong to Mickey Mouse clubs.

In Europe alone sixty newspapers beguile their readers with Mickey comic strips. Fan mail at the studio has reached a peak of eight thousand letters a week, the letters coming from every country and every town where there is a theater. Naturally, quite a few nickels are jingling into Mr. Disney's jeans today. The garret over the garage has been succeeded by a modern $150,000 studio housing a hundred employees who turn out one Mickey reel and one Silly Symphony a month. And yet—

A friend who used to know him in the old Kansas City days, when he was drawing pictures of hens and cows for farm journals, dropped in at the studio and asked him: "Well, Walt, how does it feel to be rich?"

"I don't know," Walter said, "and I don't care."

He doesn't. It's a simple truth. He lets someone else take care of all the figures. He doesn't want to know. He might begin to let his mind dwell upon figures rather than ideas, and that would spoil the fun.

Walter Disney was born December 5, 1901, on Chicago's North Side, where his father was a building contractor in a small way. His mother was the daughter of a Warren, Ohio, school teacher. The children were four boys and one girl. When Walter was five the family moved to a farm near Marceline, Missouri, and it was there that he acquired his love for animals. In the five years he spent on the farm he came to know horses, cows, ducks, chickens, all the regular roster of farm beasts, and all of them he made his pets.

His particular favorites were the colts and the pigs.

The family left the farm to try city life again in Kansas City when he was ten years old, and he got up every morning at three thirty, carried newspapers until six, went to school all day, and carried papers again in the evening, for six years. But it is really the farm that molded his character. All he recalls of his paper route is that he got to know every dog in the city. Always, in his mind, he was yearning back to the friendly animals of the farm.

There, at the age of five, he drew his first cartoon. His ink was rich, sticky, black tar, and his paper was the white side of the farmhouse—"and I got my pants warmed with a razor strap," he remembers. There, when he was not much older, he drew his first animated cartoon. He discovered, as many a small boy has, that if he drew figures in graduated poses on the margins of a book, and then thumbed the pages rapidly, the figures would move. Shortly there was not a book in the house in which he had not scrawled sketches. They weren't bad sketches, either. At least, they were good enough so that his parents did not oppose his decision, when he made it a few years later, to study art.

Today, a strange combination of ingenuousness and ingeniousness, he lives, breathes, eats and sleeps Mickey—and his notion of a holiday is to go off to a zoo with his personal eight-millimeter movie camera and photograph still more animals!

Walt Disney on Mickey Mouse's first birthday.

I Was A Showman Too!

by James J. Walker

In 1939 the volatile ex-mayor of New York, "Jimmy" Walker, talks of political showmanship and the charisma that all great leaders must have.

It was a September day in 1931 at Cannes in the south of France. The luggage was ready. The passage was booked. Everything was arranged for the start home. A chasseur—still a bellhop to me—brought a telegram. A telegram from His Britannic Majesty's Prime Minister, Ramsay MacDonald. "Surely you are not returning home without passing through London," it said. "I would be delighted if you would lunch with me and meet the members of the Cabinet." Who could say no?

I went to luncheon with the feelings of a privileged Broadway columnist, expecting the lowdown on Gandhi, the business depression, and the collapse of the pound. I got no lowdown. With characteristic good manners, my table companions concentrated the conversation upon New York. And then the ministers returned to their portfolios—and all the headaches contained in them—and the Prime Minister and I were alone in the private office at No. 10 Downing Street.

A beautiful picture—a pastoral scene—at-tracted my attention, and I asked, "Is that your own, Ramsay?" He replied, "No, it belongs to Downing Street." We both walked up to the picture and looked at it more closely. I heard its story. That led to the next picture.

Another story. And so on until the very last ——the only photograph in the room. It was small—autographed.

"You met him, Jimmy, did you not?" asked MacDonald, indicating the photograph.

"Yes," I answered.

"And what did you think of him?"

"I was deeply impressed," I answered. "Sound, thorough, sincere, and highly intelligent. A man who apparently knows his job, but very modest and quiet."

"That's just what I think of him," said MacDonald, "and I don't mind telling you we're going to help him."

The signature on that photograph was "Heinrich Bruening," then the Chancellor of the German Reich. A man of profound intelligence, of the highest purposes. A man who

105

Jimmy Walker, always a showman, posing with a girl and a horse.

became a statesman because he was a patriot. but Bruening did not last.

Why not?

Because Bruening went about the reconstruction of postwar Germany so quietly that he might have been working in secret. There were no brass bands, no clicking of heels, no spellbinding, no ballyhoo. There was something entirely missing in his make-up. Something that the German apparently must have.

Let's look back. What did Ramsay mean when he told me he was going to help Bruening? He certainly knew what postwar Germany needed. Bruening had efficiently—if quietly—made that plain. Revision of the unfairness of the Versailles Treaty, adjustments of the intolerable burden of reparations, new trade agreements, and financial aid. When MacDonald said, "we're going to help him," he could only have meant that he would help Bruening in the ways he most needed.

But MacDonald didn't have the opportunity to help Bruening. Because Bruening didn't have what it takes to hold the loyalty of the German people. He didn't understand the mass appeal of uniforms, of goose-stepping, of martial music, of propaganda, of—in a word—showmanship.

There was a man in Germany who understood those things, who was a born showman.

Adolf Hitler had all that Bruening lacked, even if he lacked almost all that Bruening had. Too often Hitler is described as a great gladiator, a daring, fearless warrior. What did he ever do that called for daring or physical courage? Was it daring for him to walk out on Geneva when France and England were crippled by their lack of armaments? Was it physically fearless for him to occupy the Rhineland when France had hardly completed her defensive Maginot Line, which she certainly could not move forward as an offensive machine of war? Did it take a warrior to win the peace at Munich? No. Hitler's success is almost entirely due to showmanship.

By showmanship he has kept his people in a perpetual state of being hopped up. It suited the German people. It suited them so much that they did not mind eating less and working more to produce a mighty war machine for their power-hungry leader to flaunt in front of less warlike nations. With that war machine in his possession, Hitler the showman could use his showmanship with more deadly effect —and even less physical courage—to get what he wanted from a world sick of war.

107

Adolf Hitler began his speeches mildly and gradually worked up to a terrifying crescendo.

Neville Chamberlain was always too much of a mathematician to bother about showmanship. When he was England's Chancellor of the Exchequer, he was the cold, hard, calculating businessman. Everything he did was according to the best traditions of solid business.

But I ask myself if Chamberlain would have survived in the past few months if he had not changed, if he had not realized that even he had to be something of a showman.

Let us look at the critical days immediately preceding Munich. The English instinct to go out and whip the bully of Europe was rising. The people didn't know they could not whip him alone. Chamberlain did know. It was no good the British lion roaring when its teeth had been pulled, until at least the new bridgework was finished. But Chamberlain had somehow to convince his people of their weakness. It was a case for showmanship, for a vivid unmistakable demonstration of the terrible possibility of air raids more devastating then London had ever known.

Why else do you think he ordered gas masks —gas masks that were, according to tests, by no means gasproof—to be distributed to all citizens? Why else do you think he ordered trenches that would have given no protection against the ammunition of a peashooter to be dug in all the parks for use as air-raid shelters? Neville Chamberlain, cold, realistic, mathematician though he is, knew that the people had not time for a thinker; that they had to have action, action and more action.

Even Chamberlain's umbrella is a piece of showmanship. It is a symbol, a symbol of peace.

No country has a monopoly on showmanship. In point of time, America belongs to the kindergarten of nations, but as far as showmanship goes we have postgraduated with honors. Barnum's circus is better known throughout the world than any circus since Emperor Claudius was a lad. And politics in the United States began where Barnum left off.

Showmanship in government doesn't have to be militant, you know. Mussolin fires his people's imagination by sticking out his chin,

Neville Chamberlain, minus his celebrated umbrella, departs to meet Hitler.

Benito Mussolini, first of the latter-day dictators, is emphasizing a point in his speech.

baring his magnificent chest acres, and showing them the way to become like the Romans of old; but it is just as easy to play upon the mass emotions with softer, more insinuating tones.

Who would you say is America's head showman? Well, my choice is immediately Franklin D. Roosevelt.

The test of a showman, just like the test of a thoroughbred race horse, is the ability to run in any kind of weather on any kind of track. He has got to be game enough to come from behind, and be philosophical when the breaks are against him. He has got to be able to go uphill as well as he can coast downhill. Franklin D. Roosevelt is way out front in the American Grand National.

In spite of a water jump in the form of a flood of editorials banging away in the biggest type in the shop at the unbalanced budget, the seven or eleven million (take your choice) out of work, a national debt of astronomical proportions, and slumping business, Roosevelt rode in a winner, with every poll, including Dr. Gallup's, showing his popularity on the increase. New Deal dividends might be low but interest in the President was high.

Cabinet officers were developing fallen arches climbing platforms to speak in answer to the mountains of resolutions denouncing

the New Deal adopted by various and sundry Chambers of Commerce, but Roosevelt, with showmanship in the form of a few slogans, achieved more than all of them put together. His opponents he tagged "economic royalists," or "malefactors of great wealth," and even those who did not know what he meant knew that he meant no good for those of whom he was talking. He followed these up with more slogans—"the nine old men," and "the horse-and-buggy era." And yet there came a time when the Master of the Slogan was himself outsloganed, when people began to shout about "packing the court" and "dictatorship" ambitions. But the President didn't call for smelling salts. He just whispered, "Bring me a fireplace."

The secret of the fireside approach is that it brings the people into one great big happy family. To 130,000,000 Americans Roosevelt gives the illusion that the family is gathered, after the guests have gone home, to talk over its intimate family problems. Daddy is talking. In soft fatherly tones he is telling the children a bedtime story, letting them in on the

F.D.R. also used rhetoric to achieve popular support.

secret of what some one older and wiser than they is doing for their welfare, and reminding them all the time that the story will always have a happy ending while Daddy is still watching over them.

Who remembers unbalanced budgets, national debts, or unemployment figures after listening to a Fireside Chat? Certainly not the

109

Fiorello H. La Guardia, another mayoral showman, enjoyed his public duties.

majority of those 130,000,000 Americans. After a Fireside Chat Franklin D. Roosevelt is no longer President of these United States. He is just a pal.

Showmanship is a mysterious quality. It is intangible, undefinable. It is like an ear for music or a mole. You either have it or you haven't it.

La Guardia is the keenest political mind that has been operating in this town in many a long day. Yet, in spite of a terrific energy and a mind that gives him a deep grasp of all municipal problems, and in spite of the fact that he has established in the public mind a reputation for honesty in public office and a sincere solicitude for the common people—in spite of those things, La Guardia cannot resist doing things as a top-flight showman would do them.

He, too, has a hat. And what a hat! Forty gallons of it, and imperial gallons at that. He has a comb and brush, like every other man. But he's different; he's not going to wear his out. His rivals talk English—good, bad, or indifferent—to the people of the city, But Fiorello is the combination cosmopolite of this most cosmopolitan city. In the ghettos he talks Yid-

dish, not because he wants to keep what he says secret but because that's the best way to be one of them. In Little Italy he talks Italian because again that makes him one of the boys. When he tells off the Germans, he can tell them off in their own language. Even when he speaks English he speaks two kinds of English which he suits to his audience—the king's English or just English.

He made a speech the other day to the graduating class of rookie policemen. It was right after the Hines conviction, and the story was topping page one of every newspaper. "Now," he said, "you won't have to take your hat off to any lousy politician any more." That was, of course, insinuating Tammany. And that was in 1939. In 1933 La Guardia had mortally wounded the Tammany Tiger. In 1937 he had killed the Tammany Tiger, he will tell you. But could he let the corpse alone? No. In 1939 he had to keep the Tammany Tiger stuffed so that—as a perfect showman —he could still do his political big-game hunting to impress the people, needlessly enough, that he was always a straight shooter.

Must every showman succeed in public life? I may be asked. Of course not. It's an asset

The Duke of Windsor, once Edward the VIII, could still find something to smile about.

but not a guaranty. Take the little man who was probably the best showman of them all. You know him as the Duke of Windsor now. But you used to know him as the Prince of Wales, the British Empire's salesman. He was royal, but showmanship made him democratic. He was popular wherever he went, and so when he visited the Americas, North and South, or Australia, he got more orders for the factories of England without asking than a whole army of traveling salesmen.

But you can't be a showman without a stage, and they took the stage away from him. Perhaps it was because he wanted to go on being a showman instead of becoming a marionette. But even at his farewell performance the great showman did his stuff at his best. That famous "At long last," broadcast to the world, was probably the greatest individual piece of showmanship that we have ever seen. And yet, was that his tops? Who know? Today, if he were entered in the European free-for-all Showmanship stakes, there are those who would lay their last dollar on Windsor to run rings around Hitler and Mussolini.

I do not maintain that success must always follow showmanship or that showman-ship must necessarily accompany success. But if the G. O. P., for instance, doesn't produce a showman pretty soon, all their complaints will be heard in Maine and Vermont.

Who are you to tell us about showmanship? some one may ask. Well, I learned about showmanship from a fellow who was mayor of New York City from 1926 to 1932. I was in his confidence, and he was given credit for putting on a pretty good show himself. In his cast were Queen Marie, Lindbergh, Admiral Byrd, the King of Siam, the Prime Minister of England, the Crown Prince of Sweden, and a host of others.

He told me that when he, as mayor of New York City, laid a cornerstone, he didn't do it to make the building more secure. He told me that when he broke ground for the construction of the Triborough Bridge, it wasn't because there was a shortage of labor. It was because he knew that all the world likes a show, and that people are so busy with their own troubles that, unless the fellow in public life shows them in a spectacular way what he is doing, they will not know he is doing it.

In other words, the fellow who isn't a showman in public life will remain a secret.

Why Civilization Will Not Crash

by Albert Einstein

Albert Einstein wrote this article in 1933, as the dark shadow of Nazidom began to spread across Europe.

The optimist affirms, the pessimist denies life. The pessimist, for all his denial, clings as a rule to the sweet habit of living. Every man at one time or another asks himself Hamlet's immortal question, "To be, or not to be?" If he decides that being is on the whole preferable to not-being, he is an optimist, even if he quotes Schopenhauer or the Biblical adage that all is vanity.

I am an optimist.

I affirm life because, whatever may be the destiny of dissolving suns and dissolving universes, there is such a thing as progress and evolution in the cycle of the human species, however brief its existence may be, measured in astronomical terms.

I am an optimist in spite of Depression, Famine, Dissatisfaction, and the Rebirth of Militarism—the Four Riders of the New Apocalypse riding in the bloody train of the World War.

I am an optimist in spite of the world-wide suppression of the rights of the individual which has followed the ambitious attempt to make the world safe for democracy. It is the battle of the individual soul to reassert itself which characterizes the epoch in which we live. No man can find his own soul until he strikes a balance in the account between himself and society at large.

If we meditate over our life and our hopes we are almost invariably faced by the discovery that nearly all our achievements and endeavors are closely intertwined with the existence of others. We notice to what extent we resemble other animals living in collective communities. The food we eat is garnered and prepared for our table by our fellows. The very clothes we wear are woven and patterned by others. Hands other than ours rear the shelter we call our home or our workshop.

Our knowledge and beliefs are mostly a heritage. They are almost entirely transmitted to us by others. Others long since gathered to their fathers have created the means by which understanding comes to our brains. Without speech our mental coffers would be empty indeed! Our intellectual horizon would hardly extend beyond that of the elephant and the ape. Language creates the brotherhood of

112

man. It is this gift, the ability to convey complex ideas and emotions to others, that differentiates the human biped from his zoölogical kinsmen.

Left entirely to himself man is more helpless than the animals. Try to picture a baby left to grow up absolutely alone from birth! The abysmal primitiveness of such a creature is beyond the scope of our imagination.

What does all this mean?

It demonstrates our dependence upon our fellows.

No matter how great or distinguished a man's gifts or potentialities may be, he is distinguished or great only in reference to his group. The individual is significant not so much as an individual but as a member of the human family. Society is the force which directs his material and spiritual ends from birth to death.

That gives us a rod by which we can measure the merits of any man. His value depends primarily upon the degree in which his emotions, his thoughts, and his actions are directed toward enriching the life of his fellow men. Good and bad are not absolute terms; as applied to a man's worth or his character they depend on his position or his attitude in his relationship to his group. Thus it would seem as if the social attributes of a man were the sole factors upon which his relative position in the scale of humanity rests.

Yet this conclusion is erroneous.

It is not consistent with the history of the human race. For if the individual depends upon society, society itself is nurtured by the riches in the individual soul. Patently all material, spiritual, and moral possessions which we receive from society at large have come to society from individual forces. Ever accumulating, ever growing, through innumerable generations, all civilization and all culture rise from the roots of creative individualism.

It was not society at large but an individual that first struck fire from flint. Some individual first conceived the thought of wresting food from the soil by growing plants. Still other individuals first envisaged the steam engine and the filament that brings us light.

Only the individual can think and, thinking, create new values for the world. Only the individual can set up new moral standards which point the way for generations to follow. Without decisive personalities thinking and creating independently, human progress is inconceivable.

The health of society depends no less on the integrity of the individual than upon the social bond which unites the individual with his group. But the indidivudal cannot grow without the background of a coöperative community. Greco-European and American culture blossomed from the seed of individual achievement. In particular the cultural flowering of the Renaissance drew its strength almost entirely from the literation and relative isolation of individual souls.

What does all this signify for us?

Let us look at the time .in which we live What is the condition of the group? What of the individual?

The population of the areas where our peculiar type of civilization prevails has increased enormously. The population of Europe alone has increased threefold in a century. In America the rate of increase has been even more prodigious. But the number of independent leaders, creators, and thinkers has decreased in inverse proportion. There are few individuals today who tower above the crowd. The few who stand out owe their distinction chiefly to some productive achievement. In the world at large organization has taken the place of individual leadership. This holds true particularly in the realm of technical achievement. It is also true in a striking degree in the domain of science.

The lack of great individualities in the world of the arts stands out with painful clearness. Painting and music especially have degenerated. Politics, too, is bankrupt. Not only are there no great politicial leaders but the individual citizen has suffered almost universally a decline in spiritual self-reliance and in his sense of justice. Yet spiritual self-reliance and a keen sense of justice on the part of the individual citizen are the two pillars on which the structure of democracy rests. Without them parliamentary systems are barren. Because the individual has lost these two prime civic virtues, democracy and its parliaments are tottering in many countries. Everywhere

A young Albert Einstein explaining his theories in a classroom.

dictatorships arise and are tolerated because the sense of dignity and individual rights is no longer sufficiently and vibrantly alive.

The masses everywhere lack independent political judgment. The public of every country can be egged within two weeks into such a degree of hate and hysteria that its individual members are ready to kill or be killed in military trappings for any special interest without regard to its merit. Propaganda creates compulsory military service, or rather compulsory military servitude. In my opinion the most shameful symptom of the lack of personal dignity from which our civilized world suffers today is its acceptance of the shackles of compulsory military service in any form. In view of these disturbing phenomena there is no dearth of prophets who proclaim the imminent collapse of Western civilization. I do not align myself with these pessimists. All signs to the contrary, I believe in a finer future. I may be permitted to substantiate briefly the reasons for my conviction.

Mankind Advances Too Fast

Mankind suffers not because it has failed to advance but because it has advanced too fast.

I attribute the present manifestations of disintegration to the fact that the growth of industry and machinery has sharpened the battle of existence to a point where it impairs the free development of the individual. Potential leaders lack the leisure which they need for their growth. The development of the machine should have produced the opposite effect. It should have diminished the demands on the individual for labor to supply the wants of the community. But the world has not adjusted itself to these changes. As a result unemployment and restlessness stalk feverishly through an unstable world. Mankind is beginning to realize that its most imperative task is a carefully planned reapportionment of labor.

Once we have accomplished this redistribution we can readjust our lives with material security and leisure for each individual. Enlivened by a new sense of security and freedom, energies now harnessed and repressed will liberate themselves in the individual soul. We shall evolve once more great personalities, able to enrich our culture life. Drawing new strength from individualities, thus mankind will regain its economic balance and its spiritual health. The very intensity of our trouble indicates the determination of the social organism and of the individual to throw off the ailment.

Future historians will construe the crisis that grips the world today as a symptom of a social malady brought about solely by the too rapid tempo of civilization. Humanity conquering its infantile disease, will strive upward and on to attain its appointed goal.

WRITERS AND WRITING

The end of World War I marked the beginning of a new era in America. So many things were changing and it only follows that these events and feelings should be reflected in our writers and writings.

Hemingway, Fitzgerald, Faulkner as well as many others were developing styles and viewpoints. All had something to say, something to impart to us.

Hemingway was the historian of the "lost" generation giving us "The Sun Also Rises," "A Farewell to Arms" and many others. Fitzgerald recorded the "jazz" age with many of his short stories.

The list could go on and on for this was the most productive literary period in our history. It stands to reason that if things are changing for us as a nation and a people, then the material is available for creative minds to chronicle. We had come of age internationally in so many areas it was only fitting that our literature should also take its place throughout the world.

There are many pieces that could be chosen to document this position and these will be collected in the two volumes on Writers and Writing. For the present, however, we have a unique literary experience. The short story that follows is by a man whose writings served to mirror the events of his country and time, yet it still retains some identification for all of us.

The story was hereto unpublished and is by a Russian author named Leo Tolstoy.

Yellow Saplings By The Lake

by Leo Tolstoy

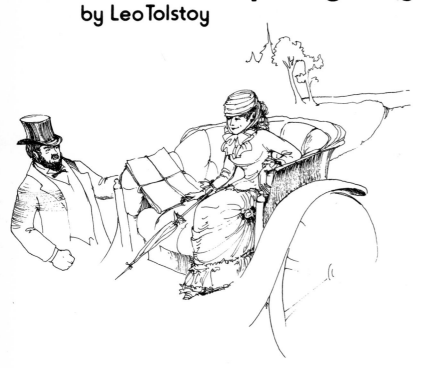

Translator's Note: *Just when this newly discovered short story by Leo Tolstoy originated cannot be told with certainty. The well-known Tolstoy scholar, N. N. Gusew, who placed it at my disposal, believes that it was written at the beginning of 1889.*

Although in itself a finished piece of work, this short story is doubtless the embryo out of which the world-renowned novel, The Kreutzer Sonata, grew some years later. In the novel, however, not only was one of the chief characters changed from an artist to a musician, but the whole work was written in an altogether different tone from the short story.

Posdnyschew had married as men do. He had studied at the university; he had also gone to work after that, and he had arrived. Then the consciousness of love awoke in him. They met.

She was young, beautiful, really very beautiful, not without dowry; she had duly attended boarding school, although she did not graduate. She had curly hair and dressed modishly. She was dainty, somewhat artless, good-natured, but, above all, nice.

"Well, what about it?" he thought. "I, too, am a human being, am I not? Outside of my chemistry there are still other joys in life: beauty, love. Why should I live only as an onlooker while others take everything they can? Also, the years are passing. I, too, have a right to live."

So he thought, and so he married. He saw the whole thing through, as is necessary; he went through the whole experience.

In earlier times, when you married only according to the will of your parents and didn't see the bride until the wedding and had had no experiences at all, everything was fine and honorable: the feather beds and the linen chest and the clothes and the wedding finery. But now, when in the souls of all who get married the physical is the most important part actually, when no one believes any more in the sacrament—and Posdnyschew is a scholar, consequently he also does not believe—all of this trousseaux, linen, dressing gowns, clothes, negligees, chocolate, etc., is distasteful at least.

Well, he went through the whole business, was married, and learned that there are some very nice experiences to be had outside of chemistry. He was pleased with it, very.

He went to work and worked, came home and in his home found grace, taste, beauty, and amusement, instead of dust and ennui. What better could one want? "Why," he thought, "didn't I think about this long ago?" And so he imagined that nothing else would ever come beside these pleasures.

But something new and unexpected came, in the first few weeks. Tears came, and discontent, and her desires for something which didn't agree with what he himself needed.

116

Something happened as always happens; what you yourself would have experienced if you had introduced a certain convenience into your home—a fireside chair in which to rest, and suddenly the chair kicks up its legs and makes demands. What demands? Why, to play a little, and to rest.

You may wonder how a chair could wish something for itself; after all, it is only—a chair. You turn the chair around, you try to sit down, and the chair does the same. So goes it among men.

Quarrels and wrangling began—and what wrangling! Such as always comes to pass among people who don't at all understand, and don't want to understand, that another's life can have its claims as well.

At first this wrangling seems surprising. How is it possible? Only six hours ago love was so strong, and suddenly nothing remains of it—the chair was so soft and comfortable, and suddenly its legs are sticking up. Love surely couldn't have been so strong when nothing remains of it now, not the slightest sign.

Be that as it may, there isn't any of it there, not even a trace. A totally strange and hateful person stands before you, and the wrangling begins. It is a secret which everyone conceals from all others, although everyone is aware of it. Quarrels and hate began just as among animals, and at that all the stronger as what was called love before was strong. Such a hate as leads frankly to the wish that she, and he himself as well, might die. And so it goes on until once again the illusion of passion overshadows everything.

In this case, also, things went on just so. But, beside all this, there came still another unexpected situation: after he had created a pleasure for himself, he failed to take into consideration that there are many other lovers of the same pleasure, including some very clever people who know not only that it is very pleasant to live with a woman, but also that it isn't necessary to have at the same time the inconveniences and disagreeablenesses which are part and parcel of married life. They know also that it is decidedly pleasanter and freer from worry to skim the cream from the milk that others have had the trouble of milking from the cow.

His wife was very beautiful; she had, you know, such a provoking and arresting beauty! Others also, the cleverer ones, had noticed that. Furthermore, one of these cleverer ones advanced to the attack.

Oh, yes, then began for Posdynschew all those questions: How to obtain the freedom that both desire? Why should a mutual understanding be destroyed when, if a strange gentleman feels the necessity of taking your arm, for example, it remains just a meaningless little arm and then go on his way. He would have three arms and I only one. And I would gladly give him my arm.

Thus began what you think should have been so easy to solve. The chief hindrance to this simple solution, however, lies in the fact that the whole problem will never be clearly stated. The devil only knows if my wife is going to be unfaithful to me, or has she been so this long time? Or has she so planned things that just today she will be unfaithful? Nobody knows, neither the husband, nor the wife, nor he who lies in wait for the other's wife.

This latter says to himself: "Well, perhaps the affair can be arranged today." He always calls it "the affair." The wife says to herself: "I am in love; the feeling is strange and nice." Whom she loves, however, she herself doesn't know. But the husband thinks: "No, it only seems so to me." A minute later he thinks: "How strange that I have never noticed that they have found each other!" And another minute later: "Still . . . perhaps not. I won't think about it." And he makes a resolution not to recall this nightmare any more.

A pleasant occupation, nightmares! He who hasn't experienced them doesn't know how hideous they are.

And so it began, and so it went on, and on, and on. Two years passed by. It turned out that the pleasure—remained a pleasure; much that was beautiful and comfortable along with it, but also much that was difficult. And how difficult!

You might say she was no educated woman! She did have just that sort of an education which permits a woman to say to herself: "I am an educated woman." If a woman speaks English, she calls all people who do not speak English uneducated; and if she—God forbid!

—has read about natural history, then all those about her are uneducated: *she* has read about it.

He had an eye for her development, gave her books to read, himself read with her. She read those books and loved to discuss them in detail, especially if that cleverer person who lay in wait for her were present.

Everything went on as usual, and everything was a sham. He knew why he had married her. Her development wasn't necessary to him, it was only custom; only superficially was he concerned about her development. She, too, knew what she was and why he needed her, and wherein her strength lay; but she only gave herself the air of being interested in still other things.

Interests she did have, poor thing, but only her face, her body, and the clothing of her body and of her children. There was a child. Well, you know, having a child, also, is so beautiful: a little crib, a bathtub, children's little clothes—these were always of interest, wherewith she could be so beautifully coquetish in the nursery. You could never decide: does she bathe the child in order to have the child clean, or to show her white elbows? Does she caress the child because she loves it, or merely to lay her beautiful head on the little head of the child?

So it went on and on; and then it seemed as though something had happened. But it happened in such fashion that no one could know if it had happened or not. Actually it was no secret for the husband. Were it a secret, it would be much easier for him; but it was that same nightmare about which no one should think if he would not tear his heart out.

You ask what happened. It was in the country; I was living there too. In Posdnyschew's neighborhood lived an artist: such a youthful, decorative person; one of those who are clever, one of those also who have their pleasure without getting married! He was twenty-eight, a handsome fellow with white skin and smoldering blue eyes, red lips, and shimmering, reddish mustache. What more do you need? He was always painting trees with little yellow leaves, had his hat and rug, and with his palette was forever changing his location. He had made the acquaintance of the Posdnys-

chew family and often visited them.

Then the spider web began to be woven around him on all sides and he ensnared himself more and more in it. The web was fine, it would be a shame to tear it, why indeed should one? One fine thread after the other, one thread after the other; hardly had he looked around before he was snared, body and soul.

She loved painting; already in boarding school she had shown great ability, but had had no guidance. After awhile she began to paint, more and more: how could she let such a good opportunity go by? He is famous, and so generous and ready to help, and, besides, he has such a pure soul! To all appearances there is no other interest beween them than high art. Oh, how beautiful this spot of color is! Ah, how green this leaf is! But should the husband show only a trace of jealousy, or begin to bare his claws, at once she is all injured innocence and asserts that she never once thought about the other one! "You, yourself, are suggesting bad thoughts to me!" The man draws in his claws, but jealousy remains.

How wonderful the attitude of these two to each other seems—their similarity of tastes, their joy of living, their joking!

The husband's presence doesn't change the simplicity of the atmosphere. He even begins to change in this atmosphere, but in his soul is hell. He can't explain all that he thinks without betraying himself. To seek an explanation from her only means unleashing all the animal instincts. To leave the question unexplained is still worse.

He had perceived the chief fact, which in all such cases is the saddest, that what she was to him—an object of pleasure for a few minutes of life—she must be in still greater degree for all other men. And what he was to her, other men offered to be in hundredfold greater degree, because of their variety and greater attractiveness. Truth to tell, then, she must prefer those others.

He, the husband, recognized no inner restraints in himself, or in her. Everything pointed to the fact that if she isn't actually stupid, she must take the step. To be sure, there are hindrances: gossip, bad reputation, unpleasantnesses; hence it was obvious that she must take it so that no one should learn of it. And if she should take it, or had already done so, he the husband, would not find it out.

No, indeed, she had not taken it! Actually, however, she had now been having an affair with the artist the whole summer long. Were he but willing to analyze his impressions exactly, he must know, know for a certainty—not as you know that of which you have visible proofs, but because of your inner impulses: a certainty, but without proofs.

I know of a characteristic episode in the life of the Posdnyschew family at that time. In order to understand it, you must try to realize their feelings as well.

One day she was going from the country into the city. She needed to get something—you know, as ladies are always needing something—very urgently. But he, the artist, was to finish painting some wonderful sapling or other by the lake. She was going into the city. She was in a hurry. She was particularly beautiful on that day, said her husband.

But she mentioned twice during the conversation that it was going to be a nuisance for her to do some sort of an errand in the city for the artist; she gave him thereby to understand that the artist was remaining in the country.

Suddenly Posdnyschew understood that everything was over. She had been unfaithful to him. He went to see the artist, but was told by a neighbor that he had gone into the city the evening before. Now he remembered her frequent trips to the city, in bad weather, and without sufficient reasons. So it had happened! She had already done it—done it just as she must have done it and remain true to her ordinary instincts.

He couldn't stay at home and decided to go to the city—not just simply to go to the city, though: he took his revolver with him to shoot his wife, and *him!*

This dreadful decision came about quite naturally; but what happened was quite otherwise. He met her on the way. He espied her from quite a distance. She was coming back home, sprightly, gay, contented. In the first moment of meeting he saw in her face that beaming happiness which was always for him the surest inner proof of her unfaithfulness.

When she noticed him she smiled, and it seemed to him that she was laughing and smiling at him at the same time. But after that she became uneasy.

"What's the matter with you? Where are you going?"

He wanted to lie, but couldn't. He got into her carriage, and in so doing he crushed the pictures which she had brought from the city. She became annoyed. As though she had a right to be angry with him!

"What's the matter with you? Are you crazy?"

"I can't go along any further."

They got out of the carriage and went home on foot.

"It's torturing me!"

"Oh, you're thinking about Leonid Nikolae-witsch? Forget it! You ought to be ashamed of yourself!"

Now the game began. A happy smile played about her lips, which she could not repress. She laughed at him. She would not deny it; she would not lower herself to make denials.

"How could anyone think such a thing? How could such nonsense torture anyone? Everything is all so fine, why wreck your life? If it tortures you so, I won't meet him any more. Although it is stupid and humiliating for me. As you will. You and your peace of mind are dearer to me than anything else."

And yet she was already unfaithful to him and intended to be so again. But he believed her, and she never seemed so beautiful to him. He never loved her so passionately. When taking his revolver in his hand, he had opened the way for the first time to animal instinct, but by so doing another animal instinct was intensified—the same, but with a different objective.

This episode was ended. She certainly didn't see the artist any more—he went traveling. The family life seemed to run smoother. Still, each was watching the other warily.

A year passed quietly. There was no jealousy, nor any grounds for it. There was only wrangling, and off and on he was in despair about it. He regretted that he had taken this torturing load upon his shoulders. There were attempts to be freed from it, and there was the consciousness that life was played out, that one must drag along with the burden to the end. Then would follow peace and reconciliation, but no inner ties. Each regarded the other as something that he needed, over which he had a right, but which had no rights of its own.

This year passed by then. Another child came. Habits took deeper root, the agreeable feelings of married life increased, but still the tortures increased also; seemingly, however, not in proportion.

Had you seen him at that time you would not have said that he was unhappy, he would not have been able to say that about himself. So it is with a man in whom a fatal disease is developing: he first learns the dreadfulness of his situation after the disease has already made its appearance.

About that which tortured him most he dared not speak, certainly not to that being who was nearest him, to his wife.

He told me later that his tortures were increased by his not knowing whether or not the last child was his or that artist's, he with the pale complexion who painted saplings on the edge of the lake. Sometimes he was persuaded one way, sometimes the other. He suffered terribly.

Why did he suffer? For this reason: because his wife was for him a sweet and tasty morsel which he greatly desired, and the sweeter the morsel was, the clearer it was to him that, logically, other men also wanted to eat up this sweet morsel, or had eaten it up, or sooner or later would eat it up.

They went traveling abroad. Her mental development seemed to progress. Still, her feelings were just the same. She knew that she was a sweet morsel and that one must preserve, protect, and augment this sweetness. That is what she did. Had she a petty and reprehensible nature? No. She was a creature like all the rest—a nice little animal, generous, sly, beautiful, and clever.

So they continued to live as average married people. Then it so happened that they spent a summer upon the estate of his brother, in quite another countryside than that of earlier days.

He began to be interested in farming. At the height of summer he was very busy.

She had acquaintances among the neighbors, among them a woman physican. A good soul, she talked much about the freedom of women.

One day he came home to fetch the flower stalks he had forgotten, being busy in the garden, and saw his wife also coming toward home.

"Where have you been?"
"I've been out walking."
"Out walking?"

He saw her face beaming, such beaming as was caused only by love, by animal love. Later he was coming from his work and met the physician; he was talking with her, one thing led to another, and she told him that the artist had arrived the week before and was living at the priest's house.

Then his wife came in to dinner, trying to conceal her expression, but she couldn't. In so doing, she seemed beautiful as never before. "She belongs to me," he thought, "yet I am not the cause of this beaming expression; but he is, the other fellow." Still he said nothing, concealed everything like a tiger; took pains to be only the more simple and natural. So he let

everything remain unexplained.

"Mine, and still not mine," he thought, and she seemed still sweeter; "not mine, and yet mine!" The more he loved her, the more he hated her, and the hate began to be stronger than the love. He loved her and lay in wait for her.

The artist didn't appear. How he tortured himself! He knew nothing, but he saw that she felt that this other one was here, near by; and she was meeting him! He dared not mention his name.

In this way a week went by. He said he was going into the city, and took his departure. En route, he sent the carriage back, and late in the evening himself came home, and saw when the artist, cautiously and looking all around, came up to the balcony door, hesitated a moment, and went quickly in.

" 'No,' I thought, 'I—I—I am Posdnyschew! A garden knife isn't good enough!' I ran to my room; there I had a dagger. I hardly remember how I got into her room. Yes, mine, my wife, my wife!"

He jumped through the window. She was almost undressed; she lifted her bare arms and remained sitting on the bed. "No, what's mine I won't give away!"

"I ran to her, stabbed her with the dagger, and tore it upward. She fell, she clung to my arm, I pulled the dagger from her. The blood ran—it sickened me. 'Die, you snake!' I struck her with my fist in the face and went into the hall where the maid and the house boy were.

" 'Quick! Notify the police! I've killed my wife.'

"I sat down in my room and smoked a cigarette. The neighbor physican came in.

" 'Go to her,' she said.

" 'What for?'

" 'Go to her.'

" 'Will she die?'

" 'Yes,' said the physician.

"A shudder convulsed me. All the better! I went to the door. She lay in bed; her bruised face was swollen, her cheeks and eyes blue. For God's sake, what have I done? I wanted to fall on my knees, I don't know why, and beg for something. She motioned to me.

" 'Forgive me! Forgive me!' she said.

"I was silent.

" 'I couldn't help it. I didn't know. I'm bad, but I'm not to blame; believe me, I'm not to blame! Forgive me! Will I really die? Can't anyone help me? I'll be so good, I'll make up . . . for everything . . .

"Where did she get those words? No one could do anything more for her. She died.

"I was put on trial. I am Posdnyschew. That stupid court acquitted me. They didn't know that I first began to love her really upon her deathbed. No, she wasn't to blame.

"Had she lived, I would have loved not only her face and her body, but herself, and have given her everything. And had I always loved her for herself and not only for her body, it wouldn't have been necessary to forgive her anything, probably."

GREAT AND LITTLE WARS

Every war has its heroes, and Sgt. Alvin York was outstanding in World War I. (Gary Cooper played him in the movies, which will help you to visualize the man.) In the shattering battle for the Argonne Forest, Cpl. York single-handedly wiped out a machine gun nest with his sharpshooting and captured over one hundred Germans. For awhile few knew of his feat, but the traveling artist Joseph Cummings Chase, in search of doughboy types to paint, heard of the exploit and alerted the top brass and the press. Suddenly York was a hero and a sergeant.

All along this boy from the Tennessee hills had kept a diary and here he expands it in his own rough, honest words. In earlier entries, he denies that he had ever been a conscientious objector before his war days. After that, you follow him as he sees comrades killed and then proceeds to "touch off" what seems to be the entire German army. World War I was rough on doughboys, and the diary of Sgt. York projects his feelings.

Some twenty years later, a different breed of fighter was waging war in the Pacific theater, where Claire Chennault had become military adviser to Generalissimo Chiang Kai Shek. Even before Pearl Harbor, the American Volunteer Group was fighting the Japanese in the air over Rangoon and other danger spots. Chennault taught his men to fight his way, and results were good at first. For a while the Americans seemed to be having their own way, but slowly the Japanese improved. When they dropped bombs, even the AVG ran for cover.

After Pearl Harbor, the American Volunteer Group became part of the American Air Corps. At war's end, General Chennault stood out as one of the rugged individualists of the conflict.

The Diary of Sergeant York

Sgt. York's rugged diary was first published in Liberty in 1928. The movie that followed more than a decade later was one of the most moving of all times.

Sergeant Alvin C. York was drafted into the army from the mountains of Tennessee. He has told how he was reassured by prayer that it was right for him to go to war, and has denied the widely circulated story that he was a conscientious objector. He tells here of the engagement that brought him international fame.

October 4th.

Argonne Forest, France.—We went on into the Argonne Forest, where we stayed overnight.

The battle of the Argonne started the night of the 28th of September. Well, we started on a hike, going on into the Argonne, and camped in the Zona Woods on October 3. The woods about here hadn't been shot up much. We hadn't yet reached the main battlegrounds. But we moved up on the 4th, and I'm telling you the woods were shot all to pieces and the ground was all torn up with shells.

October 5th.

Argonne Forest, France.—We went out on the main road and lined up and started for the front, and the Germans were shelling the road, and the airplanes was humming over our heads, and we were stumbling over dead horses and dead men, and the shells were bursting all around us.

And then it was I could see the power of God helped men if they would only trust him.

Oh, it was there I could look up and say:
"O Jesus, the great rock of foundation
Whereon my feet were set with sovereign grace.
Through shells or death with all their agitation
Thou wilt protect me if I will only trust in They grace.
Bless Thy holy name!"

Man-Made Cyclone

October 7th.

Argone Forest, France.—We lay in some little holes by the roadside all day. That night we went and stayed a little while and come back to our little holes and the shells bursting all around us. I saw men just blown up by the big German shells. So the order came for us to take hills 223 and 240 the 8th.

It was raining a little bit all day, drizzly and very damp. Lots of big shells bursting all around us. We were not up close enough for the machine guns to reach us, but airplanes were buzzing overhead most all the time, just like a lot of hornets. Lots of men were killed by the artillery fire. And lots more wounded.

We saw quite a lot of our machine gun battalion across the road from us blown up by the big shells. The woods were all mussed up and looked as if a terrible cyclone had swept through them.

But God would never be cruel enough to create a cyclone as terrible as that Argonne battle. Only man would ever think of doing

an awful thing like that. It looked like "the abomination of desolation" must look like. And all through the long night those big guns flashed and growled just like the lightning and the thunder when it storms in the mountains at home.

And, oh my, we had to pass the wounded. And some of them were on stretchers going back to the dressing stations, and some of them were lying around, moaning and twitching. And the dead were all along the road. And it was wet and cold. And it all made me think of the Bible and the story of the Anti-Christ and Armageddon.

And I'm telling you the little log cabin in Wolf Valley in old Tennessee seemed a long, long way off.

That night the orders came for us to take Hill 223. The zero hour was set for 6 o'clock, which was just before daylight. We were to go over the top, take the hill, and advance across the valley to the ridges on the other side, and take them and press on to the Decauville Railroad, which was our objective. It was a very important railroad for the Germans.

And the Lost Battlion was in there somewhere, needing help most awful bad!

Shells and Gas Masks

October 8th.

Argonne Forest, France.—So the morning of the 8th, just before daylight, we started for the hill of Châtel Chéhéry. So before we got there it got light, and the Germans sent over a heavy barrage and also gas, and we put on our gas masks and just pressed right on through those shells and got to the top of Hill 223 to where we was to start over the top at 6:10 A.M.

And they was to give us a barrage. So the time came, and no barrage, and we had to go without one. So we started over the top at 6:10 A.M., and the Germans was putting their machine guns to working all over the hill in front of us and on our left and right. So I was in support and I could see my pals getting picked off until it almost looked like there was none left.

This was our first offensive battle in the Argonne. My battalion was one of the attacking battalions. My platoon was the second.

125

We were in support of the first. We advanced just a few yards behind them. We got through the shells and the gas all right, and occupied Hill 223, which was to be our jumping-off place for the advance on the railroad. When the zero hour came, we went over the top and started our advance.

We had to charge across a valley several hundred yards wide and rush the machine gun emplacements on the ridges on the far side. And there were machine guns on the ridges on our flanks too.

It was a kind of triangular shaped valley. So you see we were getting it from the front and both flanks. Well, the first and second waves got about halfway across the valley, and then were held up by machine gun fire from the three sides. It was awful. Our losses were very heavy.

The advance was stopped and we were ordered to dig in. I don't believe our whole battalion, or even our whole division, could have taken those machine guns by a straightforward attack.

The Germans got us, and they got us right smart. They just stopped us dead in our tracks. It was hilly country with plenty of brush, and they had plenty of machine guns intrenched along those commanding ridges. And I'm telling you they were shooting straight. Our boys just went down like the long grass before the mowing machine at home. And, to make matters worse, something had happened to our artillery and we had no barrage.

So our attack just faded out. And there we were, lying down, about halfway across, and no barrage, and those German machine guns and big shells getting us hard.

I just knew that we couldn't go on again until those machine guns were mopped up. So we decided to try and get them by a surprise attack in the rear.

We figured there must have been over thirty of them, and they were hidden on the ridges about 300 yards in front and on the left of us.

An Attack From the Rear

October 8th (Continued).

So there was 17 of us boys went around on the left flank to see if we couldn't put those guns out of action. So when we went around and fell in behind those guns, we first saw two Germans with Red Cross bands on their arms. So we asked them to stop, and they did not. So one of the boys shot at them and they run back to our right. So we all run after them—

Sergeant Harry Parsons gave the command to what was left of four squads—my squad, Corporal Savage's squad, Corporal Early's, and Corporal Cutting's—to go around through the brush and try and make the surprise attack.

According to orders, we advanced through our front line and on through the brush and up the hill on the left. We went very quietly and quickly. We had to. And we took care to keep well to our left.

Without any loss and in right smart time we were across the valley and on the hill where the machine guns were emplaced. The brush and the hilly nature of the country hid us from the Germans.

We were now nearly 300 yards in front of our own front line. When we figured we were on top of the hill and on their left flank, we had a little conference.

Some of the boys wanted to attack from the flank. But Early and I and some of the others thought it would be best to go right on over the hill and jump them from the rear. We decided on this rear attack.

We opened up in skirmishing order and, flitting from brush to brush, quickly crossed over the hill and down into the gully behind. Then we suddenly swung around behind them. The first Germans we saw were two men with Red Cross bands on their arms. They jumped out of the brush in front of us and bolted like two scared rabbits.

Headquarters Captured

We called to them to surrender, and one of our boys fired and missed. And they kept on going. And we kept right after them. We wanted to capture them before they gave the alarm. We were now well behind the German trench and in the rear of the machine guns that were holding up our big advance.

We were deep in the brush and we couldn't see the Germans and they couldn't see us. But we could hear their machine guns shooting

Alvin York at home with his dad.

something awful. Savage's squad was leading, and mine, Early's, and Cutting's followed.

—and when we jumped across a little stream of water that was there, they was about 15 or 20 Germans jumped up and threw up their hands and said, "Kamerad!" So the one in charge of us boys told us not to shoot; they were going to give up anyway.

It was headquarters. There were orderlies, stretcher bearers and runners, and a major and two other officers. They were just having breakfast, and there was a mess of beef-steaks, jellies, jams, and loaf bread around. They were unarmed, all except the major.

We jumped them right smart and covered them, and told them to throw up their hands and to keep them up. And they did. I guess they thought the whole American army was in their rear. And we didn't stop to tell them anything different. No shots were fired, and there was no talking between us except when we told them to "put them up."

So by this time some of the Germans from on the hill was shooting at us. Well, I was giving them the best I had, and by this time the Germans had got their machine guns turned around and fired on us. So they killed 6 and wounded 3 of us. So that just left 8, and then we got into it right by this time. So we had a hard battle for a little while—

I don't know whether it was the German major, but one of them yelled out something in German that we couldn't understand. And then the machine guns on top swung around and opened fire on us. There were about thirty of them. They were commanding us from the hillside less than thirty yards away. They couldn't miss. And they didn't.

They killed all of Savage's squad; they got all of mine but two; they wounded Cutting and killed two of his squad; and Early's squad was well back in the brush on the extreme right and not yet under the direct fire of the machine guns, and so they escaped. All except Early. He went down with three bullets in his body. That left me in command. I was right out there in the open.

"I Don't Think I Missed a Shot"

And those machine guns were spitting fire and cutting down the undergrowth all around me something awful. And the Germans were yelling orders. You never heard such a racket in all your life. I didn't have time to dodge behind a tree or dive into the brush. I didn't even have time to kneel or lie down.

I don't know what the other boys were doing. They claim they didn't fire a shot. They said afterwards they were on the right, guarding the prisoners. And the prisoners were lying down and the machine guns had to shoot over them to get me. As soon as the machine guns opened fire on me, I began to exchange shots with them.

There were over thirty of them in continuous action, and all I could do was touch the

127

Germans off just as fast as I could. I was sharp-shooting. I don't think I missed a shot. It was no time to miss.

In order to sight me or to swing their machine guns on me, the Germans had to show their heads above the trench, and every time I saw a head I just touched it off. All the time I kept yelling at them to come down. I didn't want to kill any more than I had to. But it was they or I. And I was giving them the best I had.

Suddenly a German officer and five men jumped out of the trench and charged me with fixed bayonets. I changed to the old automatic and just touched them off too. I touched off the sixth man first, then the fifth, then the fourth, then the third, and so on. I wanted them to keep coming.

I didn't want the rear ones to see me touching off the front ones. I was afraid they would drop down and pump a volley into me.

Ninety Germans Disarmed

October 8th (Continued).

—and I got hold of the German major, and he told me if I wouldn't kill any more of them he would make them quit firing. So I told him all right, if he would do it now. So he blew a little whistle, and they quit shooting and came down and gave up.

I had killed over twenty before the German major said he would make them give up. I covered him with my automatic and told him if he didn't make them stop firing I would take off his head next. And he knew I meant it. He told me if I didn't kill him, and if I stopped shooting the others in the trench, he would make them surrender.

He blew a little whistle and they came down and began to gather around and throw down their guns and belts. All but one of them came off the hill with their hands up, and just before the one got to me he threw a little hand grenade which burst in the air in front of me.

I had to touch him off. The rest surrendered without any trouble. There were nearly 100 of them.

October 8th (Continued).

So we had about 80 or 90 Germans there disarmed, and had another line of Germans to go through to get out. So I called for my men, and one of them answered from behind a big oak tree, and the others were on my right in the brush.

So I said, "Let's git these Germans out of here."

One of my men said, "It is impossible."

So I said, "No; let's git them out."

So when my man said that, this German major said, "How many have you got?" and I said, "I have got a-plenty," and pointed my pistol at him all the time. In this battle I was using a rifle and a .45 Colt automatic pistol.

So I lined the Germans up in a line of twos, and I got between the ones in front, and I had the German major before me. So I marched them straight into those other machine guns and I got them.

The German major could speak English as well as I could. Before the war he used to work in Chicago. And I told him to keep his hands up and to line up his men in columns of twos, and to do it in double time. And he did it.

And I lined up my men that were left on either side of the column, and I told one to guard the rear. I ordered the prisoners to pick up and carry our wounded.

I took the major and placed him at the head of the column, and I got behind him and used him as a screen. I poled the automatic in his back and told him to hike. And he hiked.

The major suggested we go down a gully, but I knew that was the wrong way. And I told him we were not going down any gully. We were going straight through the German front line trenches back to the American lines.

It was their second line that I had captured. We sure did get a long way behind the German trenches! And so I marched them straight at that old German front line trench. And some more machine guns swung around and began to spit at us. I told the major to blow his whistle or I would take off his head and theirs too. So he blew his whistle and they all surrendered —all except one. I made the major order him to surrender twice. But he wouldn't. And I had to touch him off. I hated to do it. But I couldn't afford to take any chances and so I had to let him have it.

"I Had A Tolerable Few"

There were considerably over 100 prisoners now. It was a problem to get them back safely to our own lines. There were so many of them, there was danger of our own artillery mistaking us for a German counterattack and opening upon us. I sure was relieved when we ran into the relief squads that had been sent forward through the brush to help us.

October 8th (Continued).

So when I got back to my major's p.c. I had 132 prisoners.

We marched those German prisoners on back into the American lines to the battalion p.c. (post of command), and there we came to the Intelligence Department. Lieutenant Woods came out and counted 132 prisoners. And when he counted them he said, "York, have you captured the whole German army?" And I told him I had a tolerable few.

We were ordered to take them out to regimental headquarters at Châtel Chéhéry, and from there all the way back to division head-quarters, and turn them over to the military police. On the way back we were constantly under heavy shellfire and I had to double time them to get them through safely.

There was nothing to be gained by having any more of them wounded or killed. They had surrendered to me, and it was up to me to look after them. And so I did.

I had orders to report to Brigadier General Lindsey, and he said to me, "Well, York, I hear you have captured the whole damned German army." And I told him I only had 132.

After a short talk he sent us to some artillery kitchens, where we had a good warm meal. And it sure felt good. Then we rejoined our outfits and with them fought through to our objective, the Decauville Railroad.

And the Lost Battalion was able to come out that night. We cut the Germans off from their supplies when we cut that old railroad, and they withdrew and backed up.

As soon as the troopship landed the reporters streamed aboard to interview and photograph America's greatest World War I hero.

The Flying Tigers!
by Walter Pentecost as told to Alan Hynd

What the Lafayette Escadrille was to World War I, the Flying Tigers were to World War II. They were mercenaries, yet had an indomitable "esprit de corps." Their diary is short yet they paved the way for the eventual success of the United States Army Air Corps in the Pacific theatre. This excerpt is just a small insight into what happened over the China skies in 1937.

This picture shows why the American mercenaries were called "Flying Tigers."

We'll have to turn the clock back five years to understand why the Flying Tigers are constantly in the headlines today. In 1937, Major Claire L. Chennault, a rangy and silent former Louisiana schoolteacher in his fifties, was walking around with an honorable discharge from the United States Army Air Force following a flying accident in Texas. In a quarter of a century of flying, the major had learned to make a ship do everything but talk. More important, he had always remained a teacher, with the knack of imparting his knowledge to others.

China's Generalissimo, Chiang Kai-shek, heard that Major Chennault was at liberty, so he signed him up to take charge of the Central Aviation School at Hangchow. The result was that the Chinese Air Force, which had been taking quite a pasting from the Japs, began to turn the tables.

Chennault became an authority on Jap tactics and psychology. He sold Generalissimo and Mme. Chiang Kai-shek on the idea of forming an American volunteer group to fight under the Chinese flag. Madame's brother, Chinese Foreign Minister T. V. Soong, started pulling rabbits out of Washington hats. The result was that 100 Curtiss P-40s were diverted from an English shipment and arrangements were made for seventy-five crack United States army and navy pilots to resign in order to join the A.V.G. These boys, who loved the Japs like Cain loved Abel, kissed wives, sweethearts, and mothers good-by to go to town for the man who was now known as General Chennault.

The temporary headquarters of the A.V.G. was in Toungoo, about 200 miles north of Rangoon, halfway to Mandalay. The permanent headquarters was to be in Kunming, China, about 600 miles northeast of Toungoo, but General Chennault had decided not to move the boys between Japan and the United Nations. Sure he knew it was coming. We all did. In the meantime his training program could go ahead without interruption so long as the flyers were on Burmese soil, which was still neutral territory.

Temporary bamboo buildings with thatched roofs had been set up in Toungoo. Shower baths and American refrigerators and mattresses had been brought over for the pilots and the ground crews. American chefs prepared Ameri-can food, and there was a bar in the recreation building where the boys could mix their favorite American drinks. That rice liquor in the Orient takes the roof right off your mouth.

The General was a great believer in relaxation and recreation. He ordered a shipment of ping-pong and pool tables and dart boards and pin-ball and slot machines. Three baseball fields and a couple of tennis courts were laid out. It was nice and cool up in Kunming, and the General wanted everybody to keep in top-notch physical trim by getting plenty of exercise in the open.

Eight hours a day were devoted to training. From eight in the morning until noon, when it was reasonably cool in Toungoo, the boys were in the air, getting acquainted with their ships and taking radio instructions from the General. In the heat of the afternoon, from one to five, they sat in a classroom while teacher talked and drew diagrams on a blackboard.

Chennault As Coach

I always likened the General to a football coach when he did his stuff on the blackboard. He drew on long observation of Jap tactics to diagram flaws in the enemy offense and defense. "The Nips will spread out singly and take in as much sky as possible when you go after them," the General told the students. "Remember, you can't get 'em all. So when they split up, the thing to do is to pick one ship— any one—and keep on him until you've knocked him down."

"Some of you are going to die," the General told the boys one day at the close of a classroom session. There wasn't a flicker of expression on any face in the room. "The law of averages is bound to get some of you," Chennault went on. "But remember this: carelessness up there is a far greater danger than the enemy." Teacher's face lighted up. "Class dismissed," he said. "Who's on for a game of darts?"

On a dull day in December the General was playing a game of darts with Jack Newkirk, in command of the Second Squadron, when he was called to the telephone. When he returned, we could see he was boiling over at something. "Boys," he said, "the United States is in the war. Those Jap bastards pulled a sneak attack

131

on Pearl Harbor—and a good one." The General was clenching his fists as he talked. "The Third Squadron," he said, "will remain here for the time being. The First and Second will leave for Kunming at daybreak. I think we can scare up some action there."

The A.V.G. had to wait almost two weeks for good news in Kunming. On December 20 one of our spotters phoned in to say that forty bombers and thirty-five fighters, a favorite numerical combination of the Nips, were roaring toward Kunming. "At last!" one of the boys murmured.

General Chennault had a few quick words in the alert shack with Jack Newkirk and R. J. Sandell, a stock little ex-army ace in command of Number One. "Each of you take seven men," the General said. "That'll make sixteen in all." There were twenty-five flyers in each squadron; if only sixteen went up, that would leave more than twice that many on the ground. But the General was looking ahead. He could foresee the time when his boys would be outnumbered five to one, and more, day after day, and he figured they might as well get used to it right off the bat.

When Newkirk and Sandell were leaving the alert shack, Chennault spoke just four words —the same four words that he was always to use under the same circumstances: "Good luck. Be careful."

The sixteen who went up to hide in the sun that day didn't take diagrams with them, but they had them just the same, in their heads. For weeks, now, Chennault had been drumming into them from the blackboard and by radio while they were shamming in the air, the dodges and feints to use in order for one pilot to get five of the enemy. One of the tricks was a deflection shot. Instead of making a pass at an enemy ship from the rear and above, or coming up from below and letting go at the belly, the boys were to come in from the top at a right angle, especially when two or more of the Japs were flying side by side. Chennault claimed you could knock them down like tenpins that way. If the Japs weren't flying side by side, the boys were to decoy them into it by getting below and in front of them and seeming to offer themselves as good targets. When the Japs went for the bait, others of our

fellows were to come down sideways and and start squirting the juice just as the yellow guys were getting in position to open up on the ships in front of them.

Of course the business of deflection shots called for split-second timing. The pilots who were to do the squirting had to be sure to open up before the Japs got a bead on the decoys. I always compared a decoy to an acrobat at the circus who is left in mid-air by the fellow who swings away and who is supposed to be caught by a third man swinging forward. The difference was that at the circus, if the third man didn't show up on time, the fellow in the air just fell into a net; but there were no nets in Burma or China, and anyway a net wouldn't save the life of a corpse.

The boys came back from their first flight bitterly disappointed. The deflection shots had worked all right, and all the Japs had been able to do was to put some holes in our ships. But the Japs had taken a powder when they found out what they were up against. "We only got sixteen," said Jack Newkirk to the General, "and you told us not to chase them."

Things were quiet up in Kunming after December 20. The Hell's Angels crowd had meanwhile gone down to Rangoon, and battled on the 23rd and on Christmas. Nothing happened between Christmas and New Year's. Chennault wasn't being fooled. He figured the Japs were preparing a big surprise, and were probably waiting until they could mass some later and faster models for an all-out attack. They were probably plenty sore, and their squadron leaders had no doubt lost face back in Tokyo. After all, the A.V.G., with a loss of only two men and three ships, had knocked a minimum of seventy-seven Japs out of the air in only three fights, and gotten about a score more planes on the ground.

The first week in January passed without incident. The volunteers were all on edge, especially the fellows at Rangoon, where the attack was expected.

It came on the morning of the 10th and in worse form than we had been expecting. Spotters phoned in that the Japs were headed for Rangoon from three different directions. In the three groups there seemed to be about 150. They were flying new types of ships, too. The bombers were bigger and the fighters faster. We were in for it!

It was Freddie Hodges' day on. He stamped out a cigarette as he climbed in a jeep to ride out to his ship. "Good luck, Freddie," said Squadron Commander Olsen. Freddie grinned.

"Olger" Olsen, the commander of the Hell's Angels Squadron, looked with envy at the thirteen boys who were lighting out to tangle with 150 Japs. "Just my luck," he said. "Grounded, with the sky full of five-hundred-dollar bonuses."

How the A.V.G. hated those Japs!

Our thirteen were soon out of sight in the southeast. They were going to hide in the sun at 22,000, half a mile above the oncoming Japs, then drop down and break them up with passes.

The radio was silent for the next ten minutes. The battle was on. It was like the previous scraps. It could be heard from the airfield but not seen. There was no use in Olger asking how things were going and expecting an answer. The boys were probably too busy writing their initials on Jap ships, or so high they were wearing their oxygen masks, which prevented them from sending.

"This is Dupouy," were the next words that came through. Vice-Squadron Leader Parker

Dupouy, in charge of the flight, had just dropped down to 15,000 to finish off two bombers and a fighter. "But things are pretty bad," said Parker.

"How do you mean?" asked Olger. "The boys are all right, aren't they?"

Dupouy's chuckle came through the speaker. It was a heart-warming sound to hear. "Hell, yes," he said, "only these yellow bastards are taking in so much sky it's hard to keep up with 'em. They're in new Zero fighters that are plenty fast, and they've got some light bombers even faster."

"Where are you?" asked Olger.

"About seven miles southeast."

"Got many so far?"

"About twenty. But I don't think we can stop some getting through."

Olger was asking another question when Jap talk started crackling through the speaker. The enemy had a hidden radio some place near by and was sending on our wave length and jamming the air!

Dupouy was swearing and trying to shout above the Jap jammer. But the louder Parker got, the louder the Jap got. Pretty soon Parker's voice wasn't on any more and the Jap started to laugh. You've never had a real chill until you've heard a Jap laugh just after he's

A formation of P-40s somewhere over China.

pulled something. Then came silence.

Now ships could be heard high overhead. They couldn't be seen for the blinding sun, but the A.V.G. pilots could tell they were Japs from the motor sounds.

Then the boys at the field heard something else. The Japs had got through and were dropping eggs on Rangoon. It was Hodges who reported next. "This is Fearless Freddie," he said, laughing at the nickname some of us had hung on him. "I'm two miles northwest of you. I got a bomber in trouble. It's landing in a clearing. Better send out a jeep; maybe we'll take some prisoners."

"O. K., Freddie," said Olger. "How's everything going?"

"Great! We've got at least forty. But some of the buggies need first aid. You ought to see Dupouy's. It looks like a honeycomb."

Olger was asking something else when the Jap at the radio started jamming again. "Wonder what that hyena's saying?" asked Olger. The jabbering kept up. The Jap would stop once in a while to laugh and make the fellows in the alert shack see red.

Then a queer kind of sound came from the speaker. It was like shots being fired. The boys exchanged glances but said nothing. They wondered if what they hoped was happening was really taking place. Then the Jap's voice stopped abruptly in the middle of a sentence.

"That bird won't bother us any more," were the next words through the speaker.

"That you, Freddie?" asked Olger.

It was Fearless Freddie, all right. On the way back to the scrap he had spotted a Jap with a portable sending set, at the edge of the jungle a couple of miles southeast of the field, gone down, and given him the works!

The battle had been on for about three quarters of an hour when a couple of Jap bombers seemed to be over the airfield. The fellows in the shack knew what was coming. "Hey!" Olger shouted into his mike. "There's a couple right over us! Don't you guys want to have a place to land?"

"Sorry, chum," Dupouy came back, "but we can only handle five at a time. Better hold your hats."

The boys in the shack hopped outside and looked up into the blinding white sky. But it was no use, even with specially made smoked glasses that set them back twenty bucks a pair. They hadn't been craning their necks long when they heard an egg on its way down— and close. "Flatten!" said Olger, and they spread out on the ground.

The egg landed almost in the middle of the field and the alert shack looked as if it had St. Vitus' dance. Chunks of concrete flew through the air as if they had been fired from a cannon, but Lady Luck had joined the flattened dozen and they didn't even get their hair mussed. Then the Japs laid five more eggs, but they landed farther away. Olger picked himself up and grinned. "For a minute there I thought maybe they had something new in bomb sights," he said. "But they were just lucky with that first one."

Dupouy was on the radio again. "We're coming in," he said. "I think they've had enough. They're taking a powder."

A snapshot of some of the ground crew and pilots who came to China in '39 to fight the Japanese.

"Kill some time by chasing them," said Olger. "The runways are a mess. It'll take half an hour to clear them enough for you.

Olger barked a few words into the field loud-speaker and a hundred whites and Chinese in the ground crew appeared like magic from under the banyan trees. Each one of them went to work like Snow White in the house of the seven dwarfs, and pretty soon most of the debris was cleared away. The hole where the egg dropped remained, but the A.V.G. pilots could get around a little thing like that. Pancaking on a spot the size of a baseball diamond had been part of the instruction drummed into them by General Chennault.

Thirteen had gone away, and thirteen came back. As near as the fellows could figure it out, 140 Jap ships had come in in three formations from the southwest, south, and southeast. Our boys, getting the lay of the land from above, split up into three groups—two of four planes and one of five.

The Japs didn't see the volunteers coming down, and the three A.V.G. attacks were timed to the split second to open simultaneously. Freddie Hodges banked $1,000 for himself in the right angle, squirting juice from all six guns,

went into the deflection act, and bagged two bombers.

About half of the boys tallied once, and the rest of them twice, during the opening pass, and when the Japs saw a score of their ships spiraling down in smoke and flames, they went nuts. They took in as much sky as they could, and some of the bombers laid their eggs in the jungles and streaked for their base at Tavoy, 150 miles away.

Parker Dupouy's P-40 surely looked like a honeycomb. The propeller was shot so full of holes that when I examined it I couldn't figure out how it had managed to get enough bite to keep the ship up. One fellow returned with hardly enough cockpit glass to cut himself with, and his instrument board looked like something that had gone through a stone crusher.

The official bag that day was thirty-eight ships, which meant that the boys were going to cut a melon of nineteen grand. The flight leader figured they had gotten more than fifty all told, but some of the bags were not official, because they had not been witnessed, and some ships had been shot down deep in the jungles, where they could never be located.

135

GOLDEN AGE OF COMEDY

Sultry, wisecracking Mae West is a gal who knows all the answers. Why not, you'll say, since she writes all her own lines?

Mae was a veteran of vaudeville and Broadway musical revues, where she did a muscle-shaking dance called the Shimmy. She also thought sex could be funny and set about proving it by authoring a three-act play called Sex, which had a fine Broadway run.

Mae was on the crest of a wave, one of the big sensations of the Era of Wonderful Nonsense. But she had no answers (and nobody laughed) on the night a police paddy wagon pulled up to the stage entrance and halted her play in the middle of a performance. Buxom, high-style Mae was arrested and taken to night court like a common criminal. There she got a sentence of ten days in jail, plus a fine she could easily pay. She also won a million dollars of free publicity, which may have made her feel better. Still, she had to serve her sentence and the stretch behind bars caused her to think along the lines we ponder today. The way New York treated her—no wonder she went to Hollywood!

W. C. Fields and Mae West appeared together in movies, but didn't take to one another personally. That is, Mae never said to him, "C'mup and see me sometime." Top performers of opposite sexes and types, they were too busy upstaging each other to cement a lasting friendship. Mae had her own way of making people laugh, Bill Fields had his. The famed comedian with the bulbous nose loved his martinis (or any other alcoholic beverage), hated kids, and saw hostility all around him. But he read a lot, liked to fool people, and enjoyed passing his time making up a Fieldsian quiz.

Ten Days and Five Hundred Dollars

by Mae West

"Why don't you come up and see ME sometime?"

(Editor's Note: *The author of this article was the author and star of the play, Sex, which was suppressed after eleven months on Broadway. Miss West and two producers of the show were sentenced to pay fines and serve short terms in jail. She describes here her experience as an inmate of the Workhouse on Welfare Island.*)

The court attendant leaned toward me and said, "Are you feeling all right, Miss West?"

I replied, "Quite all right."

He then escorted me to the side of the courtroom, through a cage effect, then out a door, where there were a few steps leading down to another door. That door was opened and two gentlemen who stood there said, "Right this way, Miss West."

They were most courteous; they didn't want anything to happen to me before I got to Welfare Island, I guess.

I forgot about myself completely. I forgot I was there. Then the door opened and a husky fellow in a driver's cap and a dark blue flannel shirt appeared. He was quite good-looking, and seemed to be in his early twenties.

I figured that he must be the man with the Little Black Wagon.

He talked to another chap a few moments, and then added, "I'm coming back; I'm going to make a special trip." He glanced at me.

In a very short time the fellow with the cap and the flannel shirt returned. He was all ready for that special trip; yes, a *special trip*—for Mae West, star of Sex fame.

Why not? She was entitled to it! That was the least they could do for a beautiful star like Mae West—an actress who could sing, dance, write, and act a great play like Sex, that passed the play jury in June of 1926—then was closed down after they had let it run for more than eleven months.

Why did they close it down—after eleven months?

Why did they ask for a jail sentence—after they got a conviction?

A court attendant informed me that the fellow with the cap was there to take me to the city prison, and I asked him whether I could arrange to go there by taxi or in my own car.

The fellow with the cap spoke up very earnestly: "You will be private; nobody else with you. This will be a special trip."

Of course, having a good sense of humor, I smiled. The attendant got the comedy angle of it; he also smiled, and started for the door, saying, "I'll see what I can do."

My friend with the cap was disappointed; his feelings were hurt.

The court attendant returned, only to inform me that the court official who could have arranged for me to take the trip in a taxi was at luncheon and would not return for an hour, but he had arranged for the Little Black Wagon to be brought into the yard, away from spectators and cameramen.

It seems strange how many times I've watched that wagon pass, and thought how thrilling it would be to sit in it—and now I

137

had the opportunity and didn't appreciate it! Which only goes to show that when we get what we want, we don't want it.

I then thought, "Come on, let's get it over with." So my husky friend escorted me down.

A Ride in the little Black Wagon

There stood the Little Black Wagon.

I sat in a small compartment up front, near the driver. We were off—and we had the right of way *all* the way. Traffic stopped, east and west, at each and every crossing.

What a speed demon *he* was! He certainly did his stuff! It was very thrilling.

I stayed at the city prison all that night, in a very small room with bars in front and an iron cot with springs only. But the matrons were quite nice to me. They gave me new sheets, a pillow, and a few blankets.

At 7 o'clock Wednesday morning I was awakened. The iron cot had not agreed with me at all. I had pains and aches all over, and the rough unbleached muslin sheets irritated my skin. They offered me a breakfast consisting of coffee and cereal with milk.

No, I didn't care for any breakfast; the iron cot and the rough sheets were quite enough for me. Besides, 7 A.M. was much too early, and the coffee and cereal did not look so good. I dressed for my next trip—over the Queensborough Bridge at Fifty-ninth Street.

In the center of that bridge there is a huge elevator that lowers automobiles—including the Little Black Wagon—down to the island.

Stepping out of the land-gondola on wheels, I saw this marvelous, gorgeous stone structure most attractively decorated with big sheet-iron doors and plenty of barwork. The doors opened and I made my grand entrance.

On my second day on the island I received a request from a matron to visit the sick-wards. She told me that the patients were anxious to see me, many of them having cut my picture out of the newspapers. They were becoming excited and noisy, the matron said.

At first I disliked the idea of being on exhibition; but then I felt that if I could bring a little cheer to those unfortunates in the sickward, it would be rendering at least a small service to a part of the public that I am unable to serve on the stage.

I was escorted to the sick-wards by two matrons and the warden. On the way, we passed the tiers of cells in the main prison.

Suddenly there was a great uproar. Some one had passed the word along that I was coming through. Faces appeared at the barred doors and they shouted wildly in greeting.

"Here comes Mae!" they yelled, and, "How do you like the dress, Mae? How do you like the shoes?"

The warden was forced to smile at the hubbub my appearance had caused. He said:

"Can you imagine what it would be like if I had put you over here? The place would be a madhouse instead of a workhouse!"

I saw, then, that the warden, aside from his kindness in assigning me to his home, had the discipline of his prison in mind. It was all very amusing.

I also paid a visit to the narcotic ward. The inmates were women of all ages and all types. I talked with some. Each told a pitiful tale.

There was a young girl of eighteen whose father was Chinese and whose mother was a white woman. At the age of nine the girl was made to bring the opium pipe to her father when he wanted it. Curiosity urged her to try it.

When I saw her she had used all kinds of drugs. She was a physical wreck, and her body was all spotted where the poison of the drugs was coming to the surface.

These are not happy thoughts or sights, but they were vividly impressed upon me, who had never been brought into close contact with such unfortunates before. It was a unique but very horrifying experience, I assure you.

I'm not crabbing, though. The experience was worth the ten days, if I had ever wanted to get local color. I sure got it there. I'm going on writing and acting plays, you know.

The warden appeared to be sorry that I was leaving. He smiled wistfully. I thanked him for his kindness, and he said, "Come and see us again, sometime."

And I said, "Thanks, I will, but not via the Little Black Wagon."

He said, "Oh, I didn't mean *that*."

I said, "Oh, I know, but I just wanted to make sure."

The doors closed behind me. That's *my* story.

Can~You~Keep~A~Straight~Face Quiz

by W.C. Fields

W. C. Fields poked fun at everyone, including himself, in this not-so-serious quiz.

Grade yourself as follows:

35 correct . . . . Excellent
30 correct . . . . Good
25 correct . . . . Fair
20 correct . . . . Passing
Under 20 . . . . Failing

1—What brilliant comedian's real name is Claude William Dukinfield?

2—What close friend of mine, today a Hollywood legend, once said, "As a writer I am a stylist, and the most beautiful sentence I have ever heard is 'Have one on the house' "?

3—Can you name the chubby ex-burlesque funny man who became renowned for the expression, "I'm a ba-a-a-ad boy"?

4—What comedian, part Indian, said, "My folks didn't come over on the Mayflower, but they were there to meet the boat"?

5—List the three nationally known radio stars who, as a gag, ran for President of the United States.

6—When Lincoln was advised about a Cabinet, what humor writer advised him, "Fill it up with showmen, sir. Showmen is devoid of pollertics. They hain't got any principles. They know how to cater for the public. Showmen, sir, is honest men. Ef you doubt their literary ability, look at their posters. Ef you want a Cabinit as is a Cabinit, fill it up with showmen"?

7—What sensational comic, appearing in a picture called The Great Man, when asked if he liked little children, replied, "Yes, if they're well cooked"?

8—"When I was a boy of fourteen," said a famous American humorist, "my father was so ignorant I could hardly stand to have the old man around. But when I got to be twenty-one, I was astonished at how much the old man had learned in seven years!" Who was the famous American humorist?

9—Who penned an uproarious book about outhouses that made a profit of fifty dollars a word and caused his daughter to cry from embarrassment?

10—A man called the Perfect Fool contended, "What this country needs is a good five-cent nickel." Who was the Perfect Fool?

11—And, by the way, what is the popular radio name of F. Chase Taylor?

12—Who killed Technocracy with the bright crack, "Nothing you can't spell will ever work"?

13—Can you recall two make-believe comedy feuds similar to the Ben Bernie-Walter Winchell one?

14—Who's responsible for the famous gag line, "Oh, I know Clark Gable very well. I call him Clark—and he calls me 'Hey you!' "?

15—What rotund comic, handsome, intelligent, kind, tells a famous story which begins, "Mister, don't kill Tom the Old Fly! Why, once, in Upper Sandusky, I was placed in durance vile at the behest of a local black guard . . ."?

16—What renowned wit, upon being introduced to Garbo, said, "Pardon me, I didn't catch the name"?

17—Can you name the abusive runt who weighs only forty pounds, yet owns forty-five suits worth seventy-five dollars each, and says of his boss, "Ah, he is a man of rare gifts—very rare"?

18—List three popular radio comedians whose wives play opposite them on the air. And their wives, please.

19—What immortal comic stated that, if he were elected President, he would bring these two items before Congress: (*a*) Political baby-kissing must come to an end—unless the size and age of the babies can be materially increased. (*b*) Sentiment or no sentiment, Dolly Madison's wash *must* be removed from the East Room?

139

W. C. Fields played the cards close to the vest!

20—The expression "straight man" means (*a*) a person who refuses to take part in a crime; (*b*) a member of a comedy team who acts as stooge and feeds jokes; (*c*) a comedian who refuses to tell off-color stories. Which is correct?

21—Can you name the bearded sage who spouted the line, "Youth is a wonderful thing —it's a shame it has to be wasted on children"?

22—And, in everyday life, just who is Baby Snooks and who is her much harassed daddy?

23—What swell storyteller, who often writes for Liberty Magazine, repeats the gag about the radical speaker who, in the heat of a debate, cried, "I am an atheist, thank God"?

24—Who is an ex-vaudevillian with the first name of George, who courted and proposed to what female screwball for three years before she finally said "Yes"?

25—Do you recall the movie executive credited with saying at a pep meeting, "Gentlemen, I want you to know that I am not always right—but I am never wrong"?

26—One of America's truly great funny men was a professional drowner in his youth. That is, he'd pretend to drown in the ocean, then, when a crowd gathered to watch him being revived in the beach beer garden, the owner would sell more hot dogs, ice cream, and drinks, and split the profit. Know whom I'm talking about?

27—Can you name the actress (she was once a sexational leading lady of mine) who gave this classic advice, "Girls, the best way to hold a man is—in your arms"?

28—What rotund Supreme Court judge used to tell the one about the boy who killed his mother and father—then pleaded for mercy on the ground that he was an orphan?

29—Two rib ticklers have been on the radio for sixteen years, and they first got realistic ideas about Negro life by walking the streets of Harlem. Who are they?

30—Einstein's theory of relativity was once explained this way: "When you sit with a nice girl for an hour, you think it is only a minute; but when you sit on a hot stove for a minute, you think it is an hour." Who did the explaining?

31—What syndicated humorist once stated, "The narrower the mind, the broader the statement"?

said, "There are only three basic jokes, but, since the mother-in-law joke is not a joke but a very serious question, there are only two"?

33—A certain Governor of New York, asked to speak at Sing Sing, began with "My fellow citizens," then remembered the convicts weren't citizens, and said, "My fellow convicts." But that was worse. Finally he gulped and said, "Well, anyhow, I'm glad to see so many of you here." Who was he?

34—Who authored this dedication on a very funny book about golf: "To my daughter, without whose unflagging interest and constant assistance this book would not have been written in half the time"?

35—What comedian, who speaks in a dry drawl, writes his own stuff, chews tobacco, drew $100,000 for his last movie, once labeled his fellow comedians, "intellectual midgets living on borrowed minds"?

36—Recently some one misled American youth by advising them, in applying for a job, as follows: "Never show up for an interview in bare feet. Do not read a prospective employer's mail while he is questioning you as to qualifications!" Do you know the blackguard who spouted this advice?

37—Let's also see if you know the famous and humorous epitaph on an atheist's tombstone in Thurmont, Maryland. Well?

38—What publisher, insisting the word "news" was plural, wired a reporter, "Are there any news?" and received the prompt reply, "Not a new"?

39—Match a comic to each of the following bits of anatomy that have made the comics popular: (*a*) nose; (*b*) mouth; (*c*) hands.

40—What gossip columnist, creator of Mr. Mefoofsky, once confessed, "I usually get my stuff from people who promised somebody else that they would keep a secret"?

40 ANSWERS

1—Me.

2—The fabulous Wilson Mizner.

3—Lou Costello of Abbott and Costello.

4—Will Rogers.

5—Eddie Cantor, Gracie Allen, and yours truly, W. C. Fields.

6—Artemus Ward, great American humor writer, who died in 1867.

7—Ahem—me.

8—Mark Twain.

9—Chic Sale. And the book was The Specialist.

10—Ed Wynn.

11—Colonel Lemuel Q. Stoopnagle.

12—The one and only Will Rogers.

13—Feuds? What about Fred Allen and Jack Benny, or Rudy Vallee and John Barrymore, or any of eight other teams plus W. C. Fields and Charlie McCarthy?

14—Bob Hope.

15—Me. And it was Tom the Old Fly who released me from durance vile.

16—Sharp-tongued Oscar Levant.

17—Charlie McCarthy. Grrr!

18—Jack Benny, Fred Allen, George Burns. And their wives—Mary Livingstone, Portland Hoffa, and Gracie Allen.

19—Ahem—me.

20—(*b*) is the answer.

21—George Bernard Shaw.

22—Fanny Brice is Baby Snooks. Hanley Stafford is her graying father.

23—Your own Harry Hershfield. And not a bad gag either.

24—George Burns proposed to Gracie Allen for three years.

25—Good ol' Sam Goldwyn.

26—I think W. C. Fields is your man.

27—Mae West.

28—Judge William Howard Taft.

29—Amos 'n' Andy.

30—Albert Einstein himself!

31—Ted Cook of King Features.

32—George Ade. Hiya, George!

33—Governor Al Smith.

34—P. G. Wodehouse wrote that dedication in Gold Without Tears.

35—Fred Allen.

36—Oh, I wouldn't call him a blackguard. His name is Fields—W. C. Fields.

37—The epitaph reads, "Here lies an atheist —all dressed up and no place to go."

38—The one and only Horace Greeley.

39—(*a*) Schnozzle Durante or me; (*b*) Joe E. Brown or Martha Raye; (*c*) ZaSu Pitts.

40—Walter Winchell.

41—Sure, there are only forty questions, but this extra answer is in case you missed one. You can fill in with this answer to better your score, and the answer is—Me.